MEETINGS MAESTRO

HOW TO CONDUCT ENGAGING, PURPOSEFUL AND EFFECTIVE CONVERSATIONS AT WORK

ST HOOGWOUT

Limit of Liability/Disclaimer of Warranties

ISBN: 978-0-6453273-1-1

PRAISE FOR ST HOOGWOUT AND MEETINGS MAESTRO

"If you are in business, you attend meetings. This book provides a first class look at how to design your meetings to have a clear, defined purpose, to ensure participant engagement and deliver outcomes quickly. Great strategies, simple to incorporate."

— **Julie Bowden,** Director at True Colours People Solutions

"One of the biggest challenges we have in business is time. Finding time savings, getting more stuff done in less time, and not wasting time. Hoogwout's breakthrough book can help you gain back time and enable you to be more effective in an area that costs businesses dearly - meetings. The Meetings Maestro book gave me actionable, practical strategies to help slash time-wasting in meetings and convert exhausting meetings into engaging ones. You will win back time by investing in reading this book."

— **Nils Vesk,** Author of The Reinvention Sprint and Founder of the innovation agency Ideas with Legs

"Regardless of your level of experience and proficiency, Meetings Maestro is the quintessential guide to get even more out of your meetings."

— **Jeffery Wang,** Founder of Professional Development Forum

"ST articulated the Design elements of a successful meeting. Implementing the cues provided for establishing Context, building the Process, and nailing the Details helped our team to create better meetings with increased engagement and outcomes."

— **Jack de Leeuw,** Director of Melbourne Wellness

"I wish I'd had this book earlier in my career. If the thousands of meetings I'd attended and often led across the world had followed the Meeting Maestro way, we could have achieved more with less time. This is even more important with virtual meetings popping up everywhere. Meeting Maestro is now my reference for organising future meetings."

— **Mike Harley,** Managing Director at XPonential Australia New Zealand

"Too much time lost, too much purposelessness, in effectual meetings which could have been so much better had their creators read ST Hoogwout's "Meetings Maestro". ST has written a conversational, chatty, story-filled explainer on what it takes to make meetings work. He describes the simple, and sensible, processes that can be employed so meetings are run effectively and efficiently, people are and remain engaged and well-managed before, during and after the meeting, so that good decisions can then be made. ST knows his stuff and this very readable and handy guide will no doubt change the lives of the many who call meetings and attend them. "

— **Margot Foster AM BA LLB OLY,** Founder of The Boardroom School

"What's worse than too many meetings, too many ineffective meetings where no decisions are made. Meetings Maestro is your pathway to more effective meetings that deliver outcomes."

— **Glenn Tranter,** Founder at Glenn Tranter Consulting

CONTENTS

1 MEETING THE FUTURE

DRIVE PRODUCTIVITY, GROWTH WITH AN ELEVATED GAME

I was born and raised in a village in the south of the Netherlands called Middelrode. My hometown is surrounded by colourful farmlands, lush forests, and beautiful creeks. Thankfully, my parents still live in my childhood home. Many wonderful memories come to mind when I look back on my childhood.

I inherited my family's love for sports. Every waking moment after school or on the weekends, you could find me playing outside with my siblings or friends. Whether it was running or cycling around the block, playing catch, football, or hockey, I loved it all.

Sport is always more fun with others. So, whenever my siblings were too busy with other things, I would go around my neighbourhood to ask my peers to join for a game. My little blue bike was a vital tool to spread my invitations quickly. Much later, the phone simplified my gathering process. Regardless, it was an enjoyable challenge for me.

However, the magic always happened afterwards: when we were running around and having fun together.

Wonderful things can materialise when people gather: ideas that inspire the world, friendships that last forever, or kind acts that make a difference for those in need. Over the years, I have been privileged to be part of a variety of groups: in music, sports, charities, businesses, the list goes on and on. Each of these experiences shaped me and taught me vital lessons about what works when people get together and what does not.

> *I have seen it all and to tell you the truth, many meetings are dreadful: they represent the bad and ugly.*

In the business world, the most frequent get-togethers are meetings. Despite the incredible possibilities successful gatherings can open up, meetings often fail to deliver their full potential. This is a shame.

As a management consultant and workshop facilitator, I have seen the good, the bad, and the ugly when it comes to thousands of meetings over the last 15 years. I have worked with a wide range of organisations across Europe, Asia, and Australia. From small start-ups to big global organisations and from investment banks to marketing firms and anything in between. In my journey, I have played every single role when it comes to meetings: whether being insider or outsider, participant, organiser, guest speaker, or observer. I have seen it all and to tell you the truth, many meetings are dreadful: they represent the bad and ugly.

But I have also seen the good and great when it comes to meetings. I have conducted considerable research into what makes an exceptional meeting. I love facilitating meetings: seeing energy and team spirit evolve through different interactions is wonderful. It is amazing to witness participants explore opportunities to make meaningful progress and agree on the best way forward with high energy and engagement. This is the great potential that it is possible for you too also unlock.

A HUGE – AND GROWING – INVESTMENT IN MEETINGS

Meetings. They are everywhere and they come in different sizes and forms. One-on-ones, project team catch-ups, company-wide town halls and anything in between. Ranging from short five-minute meetings to multi-day retreats, they play a significant role in organisations.

A variety of companies have undertaken research into the average time spent in meetings by employees. *Harvard Business Review* (HBR) author Leslie A. Perlow interviewed hundreds of senior executives across a variety of industries about their experiences with meetings. Her findings, published in a 2017 HBR article[1], revealed that these executives spent over 50% of their workweek in meetings compared to less than 25% in the 1960s. This is a sobering increase.

According to other studies[2], overall time spent in meetings has been increasing by close to 10% annually since 2000. This increase affects employees at all organisational levels. The typical junior employee has at least 10 hours of meetings in their workweek and, overall, total time spent in meetings increases with seniority. Most executives are locked in back-to-back meetings which leave little desk-time to get tasks or critical thinking done.

Meetings consume more time than you might think. Just as factories use setup time to configure machines to create different parts, meetings require setup time from participants. This could be travel time, review of pre-read materials, or getting in the right mindset ahead of the gathering. Equally, after a focused meeting, participants need time to reset before getting stuck in the next task or meeting. So, setup and reset time add to the overall meeting process. An extra reason to make sure all meetings are on-point.

And this is just at work. Outside of work, people are involved in their local sports club, a passion project, and family matters also require group discussions to solve challenges and make decisions.

Meetings are an integral part of life. For anyone looking to progress in their career, an increase, rather than a decrease, in meeting time can be anticipated.

But is this time well spent?

Most meetings are inadequate, therefore more time and money is wasted!

If meetings achieve desired outcomes consistently, there is no need to question their quality. However, how are meetings perceived by executives?

From mid-2020 to early 2021, I delved into this question through extensive review of online articles and literature and by conducting my own survey and follow-up interviews.

The answer was clear: in most organisations, meetings are inadequate or even dreadful.

A variety of statistics on meetings are available online. In Perlow's HBR article, 71% of the senior executives interviewed across a range of industries indicated meetings are inefficient and unproductive. Similar research conducted by organisations[3] like Atlassian, Doodle, Booqed and Bettermeetings underlines this statement:[4]

I polled hundreds of office-based executives across public and private sector organisations in Sydney about their perception and biggest pet peeves when it comes to meetings.

More than 60% of the respondents shared that they spend at least 15 hours and sometimes even more than 25 hours in meetings each week. Only half of that time is considered as productive and well-organised.

In follow-up interviews, participants shared with me their biggest meeting frustrations from two separate viewpoints: from being a meeting facilitator or from being an attendee.

For example, Samantha, a project manager at a Sydney-based construction firm, told me: "It drives me crazy when I send out an agenda and materials, but my invitees don't take the time to read the materials beforehand. We end up wasting time to recap the situation that could have been better utilised to make decisions and progress!" She is not alone. Poor preparation by participants can be annoying. Especially when it is already difficult to get the right people in a room together in the first place.

Attendees come in with their own agendas, personality traits, and moods.

Equally, participants struggle with the performance of meeting organisers. My friend Tony, a successful executive in a telecommunications organisation, shared: "what is so hard about putting the meeting purpose clearly into the invite?" Sometimes, organisers just sent a blank invite with a vague, non-descriptive subject line. Then, invitees struggle to decide whether to attend or not.

Another common challenge gathers around expectations of how to behave in a constructive manner in meetings. It seems that every single person has a different understanding of what is common sense and proper behaviour depending on their background and experience. So, when people are in the room together, dealing with these challenging group dynamics is often a big challenge. Attendees come in with their own agendas, personality traits, and moods. Each element influences the nature and dynamics of the meeting. It can be a real struggle for facilitators to juggle the different viewpoints and behaviours, and then channel them into a productive discussion.

Today, many meetings are technology-based rather than face-to-face gatherings. And whilst video and phone calls allow for more flexibility, meeting quality becomes an even bigger challenge. Without being in the room together, participants experience many distractions that can diminish the focus and presence needed to get the best outcomes.

It can be easy to point fingers and villainise meeting organisers for woeful, directionless meetings. However, the organiser of one meeting is the attendee in another one. So, it is not that simple.

Overall, a variety of factors cause meetings to fail and this is harming the productivity of individuals and teams.

EXECUTIVES STRUGGLE TO PERFORM AND MAKE THE PROGRESS THEY WANT

As a result of the volume and inadequacy of meetings, executives struggle. Their work normally revolves around urgent priorities and, unfortunately, a never-ending and growing list of things to do. Time is a scarce resource.

When they attend meetings, executives are unable to tackle other tasks. I remember many instances where I walked away from ineffective, long talkfests thinking "oh boy, I could have completed more important tasks!" It is hard to keep your head above water when you are running from one meeting to another without being able to tick off important tasks.

Quiet desk time is vital to think, analyse data, or write an important report. Whilst a meeting might be vital, attendance from each participant is not always essential. Often, participants are invited on autopilot without consideration of whether their time could be more wisely utilised elsewhere. Meetings cost money. Salaries of participants are invested in meetings. It may not sound like a lot for a single meeting, but on an annual basis, these costs add up tremendously for organisations.

Not to mention the strain on mental wellbeing, because of the stress and frustrations from poor meetings and a never-ending task list.

The bottom line is that more time, resources, and energy are wasted in meetings that are deemed inadequate.

If executives are unable to get on top of things, they will struggle to execute their responsibilities as pressures from senior stakeholders build up over time. To survive in their existing role, and more importantly, to succeed in the achievement of their longer-term career goals, executives need a solution to address the bane of their workplace existence. They need a success recipe to prepare and deliver exceptional meetings every single time!

What is the quality of your meetings today?

Before jumping into the solution, let's take a moment to pause. Where are you – what is the quality of your meetings today?

There are four critical elements to assess the quality of your meetings:

- **Clear objectives** – Does your meeting have a clear purpose and specific objectives to achieve?
- **Relevant participants** – Have you invited relevant participants who each have a clear role and can add value?
- **Focused discussion** – Are you able to manage time effectively, maintain engaged and focused discussion on the right topics throughout?
- **Agreed actions** – Are you able to agree on specific next steps and ownership with your audience?

Depending on how well you fair with these elements, your meetings could be at three different levels.

'In the dark' meetings fail where it matters most: lack of clear agenda, relevant participants, productive discussion and agreed next steps. If you ever felt drained after a meeting, likely, you just finished an 'in the dark' meeting.

Instead, an 'on the money' meeting succeeds on all these criteria. Typically, participants feel invigorated and agree time was well spent and great progress made. These meetings thrive from different perspectives that strengthen problem-solving and decision-making. People build deeper connections and engagement increases. Exceptional meetings spark incredible results, both for teams and individual employees. Then, they underpin amazing team spirit, ownership and ultimately performance!

CRITERIA	ROOKIES consistently deliver 'IN THE DARK' meetings:	EXPERTS consistently deliver 'ON THE MONEY' meetings:
Objectives?	• Define ambiguous or no objectives	• Define clear objectives beforehand
Participants?	• Invite everybody without consideration	• Invite relevant, value-adding participants only
Discussion?	• Hope for the best	• Facilitate a focused discussion
Actions?	• Assume everyone is on the same page	• Agree specific next steps before wrapping up
Results?	☹ 😟	😀 😀 😀

Many meetings are inconsistent. They do well on certain elements, and poor on others. These meetings are 'hit 'n miss'.

So where are you, what type of meetings do you typically lead? Based on the quality of your meetings, determine your current skill level:

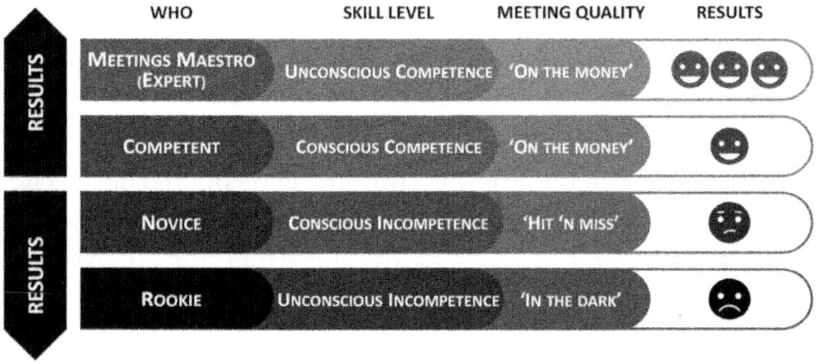

© ST Hoogwout 2021

To get on top of things and achieve the best outcomes, you need to become a Meetings Maestro. A Meetings Maestro is a person who conducts engaging, purposeful and effective meetings with ease and elegance. Not only that, they help their peers lift up their 'meeting games' too. So, entire teams can benefit.

Being competent is not enough. Most executives spend half of their meeting time in meetings organised by them, whilst the other half is organised by others. In order to get the best results, you pick up your 'meeting game' as well as help others around you grow as well so that the entire team can benefit.

So, what is the solution to increase your skill level and progress toward becoming a Meetings Maestro?

The solution: Adopt the Design-Deliver-Develop system!

Think of McDonald's and their incredible accomplishments. Each product tastes the same in each branch across the country:

burgers, fries, chicken nuggets, and so forth. McDonald's has mastered a success system that is followed by each store.

Similarly to fix meetings, you need to master a success recipe, a system that will deliver great results every single time.

This book is for executives who have had enough of woeful, directionless meetings and instead want to improve their 'meeting game' and deliver better outcomes. From my research and experience, I have created a step-by-step process that you can follow to deliver exceptional 'on-the-money' meetings every single time: the Design-Deliver-Develop system. Each of the sections and chapters is part of a tried-and-tested success recipe you can use to conduct engaging, purposeful, and effective meetings at work, like a true maestro with ease and elegance.

You need to master a success recipe, a system that will deliver great results every single time.

In Part 1 – Design, learn how to design and schedule meetings smarter. Make sure that a meeting is necessary and relevant before putting together a clear meeting process and sending out invites.

In Part 2 – Deliver, learn how to deliver exceptional meetings that achieve outcomes. It is not enough to have the right people in the room. You need to be able to manage the energy from start to finish to deliver the best possible results.

Then, in the closing section of this book, Part 3 – Develop, learn how to establish a mindset and process for continuous improvement. Every meeting provides ample opportunities for you to become a Meetings Maestro faster. Reap the benefits by following the recommended growth process.

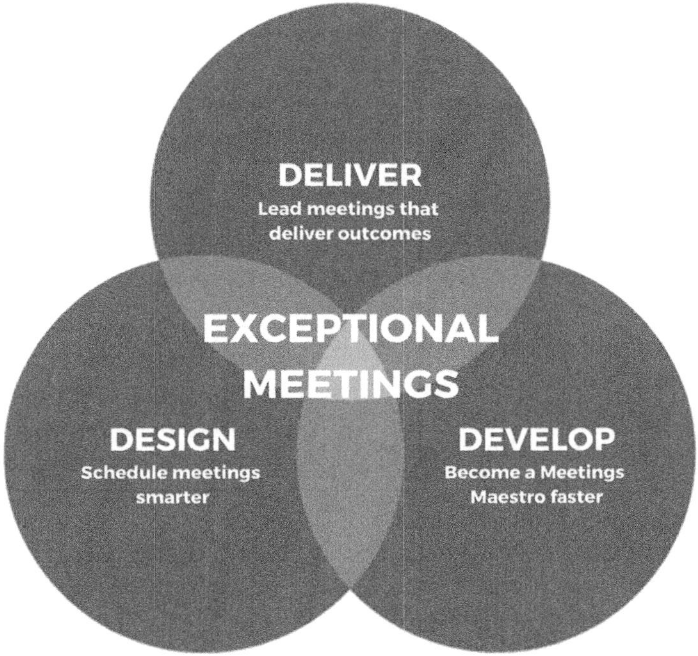

© ST Hoogwout 2021

By embracing the Design-Deliver-Develop system, you can hit two birds with one stone. First, you will free up time because of a reduction in the volume and duration of meetings in your team. Second, you will improve the quality of discussion and progress made in your meetings, enabling you to progress projects and reach critical decisions faster.

There are additional benefits. Being able to deliver one meeting well means that you can deliver multiple meetings well. Being able to deliver many meetings well means that you can lead people, deliver projects, and achieve desired outcomes. These vital skills will be recognised by peers and senior executives and unlock career opportunities.

Not only that, your ability to lead meetings well will also make you a better meeting participant. Your peers can benefit from your increased skills and ensure that their meetings improve over time as well.

This is what it means to be a true Meetings Maestro: someone who also helps others improve their meeting game so that you can benefit from well-oiled meetings whether you organise them or not.

Action Items

Meeting The Future — Drive productivity, growth with an elevated game

Review the quality of meetings in your organisation today by answering these questions:

1. *How much time did you spend in meetings over the last 2 weeks?*
2. *Consider the most effective meeting(s), what went particularly well?*
3. *Consider the least effective meeting(s), what went particularly poorly?*
4. *What is the quality of your meetings typically (e.g., in the dark, hit 'n miss, on the money)?*
5. *What is your skill level when it comes to meetings?*

By answering these questions, you understand the size of the problem that poor meetings represent in your organisation.

Read on, and learn the Design, Deliver, and Develop success recipe to deliver exceptional meetings.

IN A NUTSHELL

Whether conducted in-person or online, meetings offer enormous potential when done right. The quality of meetings reflects the quality of problem-solving, decision-making and communication in organisations. Despite their potential, the reality is that most meetings fail to be engaging, purposeful, and effective.

The antidote to poor meetings is to strive to become a Meetings Maestro. Now that you have assessed the size of the problem in your team, it is time to jump in and start learning the Design–Deliver–Develop system to deliver improved outcomes. By putting the concepts and exercises to practice and sharing with your peers, you will fast-track your productivity by fixing your meetings.

Remember that, like going to the gym, you need to do the work. You can make 'On the money' meetings the norm. But only if you put in time and effort to learn and practice the concepts outlined in this book.

In Part 1, you will learn the critical steps to design and schedule meetings smarter. Dive in, read on, and remember to share your learnings with your peers.

NOTES

1 Leslie A. Perlow, Constance Noonan Hadley, and Eunice Pun. "Stop the Meeting Madness." July-August 2017, https://hbr.org/2017/07/stop-the-meeting-madness.

2 "Minutes (Wasted) of Meeting: 50 Shocking Meeting Statistics," Booqed. Accessed 15 February, 2021. https://www.booqed.com/blog/minutes-wasted-of-meeting-50-shocking-meeting-statistics

3 "Shocking Meeting Statistics in 2020 That Will Take You By Surprise," Otter, accessed 15 February, 2021. https://blog.otter.ai/meeting-statistics/

"Meetings Statistics," Better Meetings, accessed 15 February, 2021, https://bettermeetings.expert/meeting-statistics/

"You waste a lot of time at work," Atlassian, accessed 24 August, 2021. https://www.atlassian.com/time-wasting-at-work-infographic

4 "Minutes (Wasted) of Meeting: 50 Shocking Meeting Statistics," Booqed, Biggest Meeting Irritations diagram by Doodle (2019). Accessed 15 February, 2021. https://www.booqed.com/blog/minutes-wasted-of-meeting-50-shocking-meeting-statistics

PART 1 — DESIGN

SCHEDULE MEETINGS SMARTER

2 FIRST THINGS FIRST

NAIL THE CONTEXT OF YOUR MEETING

A few years ago, I caught up with an acquaintance, Jack, in Sydney. We had met at a speed networking event, where we shared a great first connection and agreed to meet for a follow-up conversation. We met at a café in the city and started chatting. Our catch-up started friendly and casual. Then, after a few minutes, Jack grabbed his laptop saying that he wanted to show me something. Over the next 30 minutes, he made a sales presentation. Jack shared how he could help me save money on my energy bills.

I felt completely blind-sided. I had assumed we would meet to get to know each other better and explore how we could support each other's businesses without directly selling to each other. I was getting more frustrated by the minute. However, I was too polite to say anything or walk out.

From that point forward, I vowed to be extra careful about meeting people without a clear agenda. I realised the importance of making sure I was clear on the agenda and to prevent uncomfortable experiences.

Context matters!

The best meetings are those that are carefully thought through before they even appear in a calendar. Employees already face calendar overload. They spend more time in meetings as opposed to doing anything else. Often, the meetings deliver suboptimal outcomes and waste time.

So, make your meetings count. Re-think standing meetings already in your calendar, especially those that recur weekly or monthly, and scrutinise proposed meetings to determine an actual need. Preparation clarifies whether a meeting is needed and, if it is, how to best utilise collective meeting time. First things first; focus on the right areas.

The best meetings are those that are carefully thought through before they even appear in a calendar.

Imagine you are about to plan a holiday. Do you start with a detailed itinerary of each day? This is unlikely. Instead, you first identify what the main reason for your holiday is. If you are exhausted, you probably just want to relax. If you feel curious, perhaps you want to explore a new country and culture. Once you know the purpose of your holiday, you can figure out where to go and when. Knowing where to go helps find transport requirements and your accommodation. Only then can you outline a detailed itinerary of each day, if desired.

Scheduling meetings smarter works the same. Do not start with the details of when and where to meet. Instead, first things first and nail the context of your meeting:

1. **Why** are we meeting?
2. **What** are the key discussion points?
3. **Who** needs to be there?

When you answer these questions, you lay the foundation for an exceptional meeting that delivers outcomes. You might argue it is too time-consuming to prepare for each meeting to that level of detail. But, like riding a bicycle, once you get used to this process, it becomes second nature for you. The benefits outweigh the costs; make every minute count and deliver great outcomes.

START WITH WHY – ASSESS THE NEED AND PURPOSE OF YOUR MEETING

In July 2011, I achieved a major milestone by securing my first professional job as a business analyst at a consulting firm in Australia. Consulting is a fast-paced environment. Clients demand quick results, so it is important to hit the ground running and get things done.

I realised the importance of personal development to fast-track my career goals and climb up the consulting ladder. My priority was to increase my confidence and presentation skills. Thankfully, my friend, Ahmed, invited me to join the international organisation Toastmasters.

The Toastmasters' curriculum teaches members how to prepare speeches step-by-step. During regular meetings, members practice communication and leadership roles in a safe and supportive environment.

My first lesson in writing an excellent monologue was to first define a clear purpose for the speech. Purpose comes first. There are two elements to consider: general and specific purpose.

The **general purpose** is the predominant theme of your meeting. The **specific purpose** is a one-line elevator pitch that summarises the specifics of your general purpose.

My first speech in Toastmasters was called 'Black Fuel'. The general purpose was to *inform,* and the specific purpose was to inform the audience about the history of coffee.

What I learned about speech writing from Toastmasters applies to preparation of meetings. Start with why. First, define the purpose of your meeting. Without this, meetings fail to use time well and deliver the intended outcomes.

Purpose clarifies whether you need to meet. Too often, meetings have become a default. People put time in the calendar without much thinking. Sometimes, it is possible to deliver outcomes through an alternative method. The worst thing for participants is to rock up for a meeting that could have been addressed via a quick phone call between two key people, a survey, or through an email.

Start with why. First, define the purpose of your meeting.

Meetings have a time and place. They are time-consuming and require the alignment of multiple calendars and use of precious time. So, if you seek to organise a meeting, prepare using the following questions to get greater clarity first.

Step 1: What is the *general* purpose?

Before doing anything else, first consider the ultimate purpose of your meeting. Ask yourself, what is the ideal scenario for you at the end of the meeting.

'Begin with the end in mind', American motivational author Stephen R. Covey shares in his classic book The Seven 7 Habits of Highly Effective People[1]. When you have a clear end in mind, you can work backwards and decide on the steps required to reach your desired outcome.

> *Ask yourself, what is the ideal scenario for you at the end of the meeting.*

So, what is your destination? What is the purpose of your meeting? How does it fit in with your priorities and role? Are you working toward a decision, are you looking to generate ideas to move forward, are you looking to manage performance, or are you providing an update to a group of people?

There are four types of general purposes when it comes to meetings, whether between two people or an entire group. Within each general purpose, there are different meeting types.

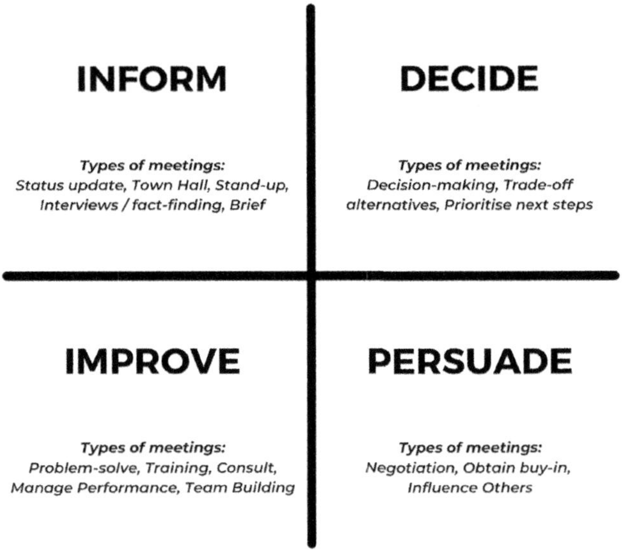

© ST Hoogwout 2021

It is possible that you seek to inform your audience and decide on a particular topic. In this case, consider the ultimate purpose of your meeting and select the single purpose that fits best.

For example, say your organisation is implementing a new timesheet system. Whilst you want to inform your staff of the upcoming change, it is important that you persuade them to use the new system from the launch date. Persuasion requires a different agenda and information than what a simple update calls for.

There are exceptions. Many organisations conduct team retreats that last one or multiple days once or twice a year. These events often contain segments with a different focus during the day. For example, team-building activities, financial performance updates, strategy brainstorms, and so forth. If you are organising a similar event, consider each segment as a separate meeting with a unique purpose and plan accordingly.

Step 2: What is the *specific* purpose?

What if I asked you to draw a house on a piece of paper? How would you go about it? If you are like me, you might start with a square or rectangle and then put a triangle on top for the roof. If you are a more skilled drawer, you might bring the picture to life with beautiful three-dimensional flavours. How many doors and windows would you add? Would you also include a chimney, a balcony, or even a carpark to make it look like a real house?

If you were to take your finished picture to a developer, would this person be able to start building your house?

The general purpose is your basic drawing of your house. It is a great starting point; however, it is not enough to conduct a stellar meeting.

Now that you have clarity on your general meeting purpose, expand it into a specific purpose. The specific purpose is a one-line summary of what your meeting seeks to achieve. The word specific is crucial, make it as specific as possible to set yourself up for success. Here are some examples:

General Purpose	Specific Purpose Examples
INFORM	• *Inform all employees on the new working from home policy* • *Inform your team on a change in project scope* • *Inform the organisation on the financial year results*
IMPROVE	• *Brainstorm how to improve productivity of the team* • *Discuss how to resolve issues between colleagues* • *Define alternative approaches to realise project outcomes*
DECIDE	• *Decide service offerings to pursue for increased revenue* • *Prioritise next steps to obtain buy-in for a new project* • *Select the best candidate to fill a critical vacancy*
PERSUADE	• *Persuade the finance team to participate in a pilot project* • *Convince a colleague to take on additional workload* • *Use stats to highlight the need to resolve a workplace issue*

Added detail will simplify preparation and improve meeting performance. Consider the following specific purpose example: "*Persuade the finance team to participate in a pilot project*". The statement is a good starting point. Strengthen it by adding details: "*Persuade the Finance Director of the benefits of obtaining improved accuracy and timeliness of invoice data by participating in the pilot of the new invoice system*".

With the added details, you obtain greater clarity which helps to streamline the rest of your preparation.

Step 3: Is your meeting critical now; does it fit your team strategy?

My friend Chris specialises in office design. By changing the layout of workspaces, he helps organisations improve productivity and employee satisfaction. Chris' weekly routine was to discuss with teams their current and desired office working environment and how to realise the change. I can just imagine discussions around the need for open office space versus more segmented spaces where people can focus and get work done. Or what about the need for plants for improved air quality and big windows to let in natural light?

> *Now that you have defined your general and specific purpose for your meeting, pause and reflect on whether the meeting is critical now.*

These discussions mattered. Until early 2020. Then, the COVID-19 pandemic arrived in Australia and the federal government ordered a lockdown requiring office workers to toil from home. Instead, Chris had to rapidly shift and now supports colleagues in creating a productive atmosphere for working from home.

Criticality can change quickly due to a shift in priorities. Does it fit with your organisation's vision and strategy? Is it critical to achieve your specific purpose now?

If yes, go ahead with your meeting preparation. If the answer is no or you are not sure, assess any changes to be made.

Also, take the opportunity to re-think any existing meetings in your calendar, especially those that recur frequently. Meetings are an investment of collective thinking time. Not dissimilar to a loan, you are borrowing time and experience of invitees. So, make sure that the meeting focuses on a worthwhile purpose and objectives. As opposed to a waste.

Step 4: Could you achieve this specific purpose without meeting? How?

Sabil is a partner at a Sydney private equity firm. Meetings are unavoidable for him. It is common that he is swamped in back-to-back meetings from 9 to 5 with little time to breathe, take a break, and get other work done. "You know what I hate," he told me, "Meetings that could have been resolved by email or with fewer people."

Often, objectives can be resolved without meeting, which saves precious time.

In many organisations, people organise meetings on autopilot. Time adds up. Often, objectives can be resolved without meeting, which saves precious time. People tend to have a 'Let's meet' mindset. Challenge this mindset to stop wasting time. Consider your purpose in a different light.

How can you achieve your purpose without gathering?

There is a time and a place for meetings, and this is not about removing them altogether. This question challenges the 'Let's meet' mindset to re-think intelligent ways of achieving goals and investing time.

A simple email, quick phone call, or team poll can often be a smarter alternative to obtaining people's input without a separate meeting.

Step 5: Given your answers so far, is there still a real need to conduct your meeting now?

A few years back, I was delivering a project for the state government. The project had a mandate from the top and was to be rolled out across the different government departments. To solidify buy-in from each department, I organised introduction meetings with relevant stakeholders. During these sessions, I would present the project background, objectives, and desired support from each department.

One of the worst experiences I had was when the most important attendee did not show up. There is no point in driving a change if senior stakeholders are not present and bought in. Somehow, even though I was sure about the criticality of this meeting, this person was not aware of the mandate and did not agree on the level of urgency. It took me a lot of extra effort to obtain the required insights from that person. Don't make this mistake. Instead, ensure meetings contain a compelling message for your audience to avoid a similar challenge.

Ensure meetings contain a compelling message for your audience.

Now that you have reviewed and answered each of the questions so far, are you sure there is still a real need to conduct your meeting at this stage?

If so, great. This process is designed to help you identify a clear purpose, make sure your meeting is critical for your attendees, and that you have exhausted all avenues to achieve this purpose.

With a real need and clear purpose for your meeting, continue with the preparation to translate your why to what, purpose to objectives. You are on track to make sure the right people will attend your meeting and avoid the wasted opportunity I experienced in the example above.

Action Items

Start with Why – Assess the real need and purpose for your meeting

Answer the following questions for each meeting you organise:

1. *What is the general purpose for your meeting?*
2. *What is the specific purpose for your meeting?*
3. *Is your meeting critical now for all attendees; does this purpose fit in with the strategy of your team?*
4. *If you could achieve this specific purpose without meeting, how would you do it?*
5. *Given your answers so far, is there still a real need to conduct your meeting at this stage?*

If your answer to question 5 is yes, please go ahead with your preparation.

If no, then re-assess what tweaks you need to make or put a pause on this meeting and achieve your desired purpose without meeting.

TRANSLATE WHY TO WHAT – DISTIL KEY OBJECTIVES FROM THE MEETING PURPOSE

Writing a book is not easy. I found writing this book one of the most challenging and even frustrating projects I have ever worked on. To get the structure right was especially time-consuming. From the start, I was clear about my general and specific purpose for writing this book:

"To persuade leaders to use a more intelligent methodology to prepare and lead meetings that realise personal and organisational outcomes quicker and smarter".

But a 'purpose'-one-liner does not equal a complete book. Also, the specific purpose for a meeting does not contain a complete roadmap for successful meeting preparation. It is a foundation that needs to be fleshed out to tell a clear story.

Next, it is time to translate Why to What, translate the specific purpose into key meeting outcomes. Objectives directly inform the agenda of a meeting. They form the key building blocks. Without a clear and coherent meeting story line, attendees get lost, and time is wasted. Instead, distil key objectives from your specific purpose that bring participants on a logical journey.

Each meeting is different and specific objectives depend on what you seek to achieve. However, there is a valuable framework to define objectives well. Early in my consulting career, I learned the 'Situation-Complication-Questions-Answers'-framework (SCQA). The SCQA framework was adopted from the work of American management consultant and problem-solver Barbara Minto[2] and is useful for structured thinking and problem-solving.

To help translate your specific purpose to key objectives, I have adapted the SCQA framework into a SCORE model.

SCORE Model		Potential Agenda
S	SITUATION	
		(1) Introduce the current situation and challenges that need to be resolved
C	COMPLICATION	
O	OPPORTUNITIES	(2) Discuss opportunities that might address the current challenges
R	RESOLVE	
		3) Agree specific next steps to resolve and wrap up the meeting
E	END	

Objective #1 – Situation & Complication

In 2018, Marvel Studios released their superhero epic Avengers: Infinity War. The studios had successfully launched the 'Marvel Cinematic Universe' (MCU) with Iron Man in 2008. Since then, the studios went from strength to strength with every subsequent movie, achieving both commercial and critical acclaim. Infinity War was the studio's most ambitious project to date. It brought together a massive ensemble of stars and storylines from the preceding 18 movies into a grand finale.

My wife, Mariam, and our friend, Bruno, watched it together and we absolutely loved it. Even though many people loved it, critics agreed on a key point. The movie was not a standalone experience. To fully understand and enjoy it, someone needed to watch the 18 MCU-movies first.

Similarly, an effective meeting does not rush in. Attendees may not be intimately familiar with the topic at hand. The first objective for a meeting is to provide a brief recap of the situation and complication. The Situation provides background on the topic in terms of key facts people can agree on. The Complication highlights changes in the situation and informs why the topic needs a discussion in your meeting.

Objective #2 – Opportunities

"To have one choice, is no choice at all.

To have two choices is a dilemma.

And to have three choices offers new possibilities."[3]

American psychotherapist Virginia Satir specialised in the field of family therapy. Couples or families would visit her to resolve issues and strains on their relationships. I love her work. The quote above summarises her 'Rule of Three': Satir would encourage people to always consider at least three choices to address a particular situation.

The first objective in meetings is to introduce the current situation and challenges that need to be resolved. Next, present and explore different opportunities that can address the situation.

It depends on your general purpose how this section is structured. When persuading or informing an audience, a decision was already made. Now, you need to bring your audience on the journey.

Highlight the pros and cons of each possibility. Let your audience know thorough work was completed to come to the decision.

When the purpose of a meeting is to improve something, you may brainstorm different opportunities with colleagues. Do not present just one solution. Instead, the objective of Opportunities is to consider multiple solutions to a particular situation.

Objective #3 – Resolve and End

In the opening story, I shared my unfortunate encounter with Jack. During his sales pitch, a million thoughts ran through my head: "Shall I stop him and tell him this is inappropriate?" "Shall I just walk out?" "How can I make it stop?"

In the end, I was polite and waited through his pitch. We said goodbye and I never saw him again. What if I had stormed out in frustration? I assume Jack would be surprised. I would still be annoyed. But the meeting did not have a natural end. It was like finishing a movie without a conclusion.

Humans crave clear endings and beginnings. Equally, meetings need a clear ending. If not, time is wasted. Prevent this through the third objective in the SCORE Framework: Resolve and End your meeting in the best possible way. Before you wrap up, agree upon clear next steps and timings, assign responsibilities, and avoid misinterpretation by attendees. Then, close the meeting.

> *Clarity is key to achieving great outcomes. Next, ensure the right people are invited to the meeting.*

Of course, every meeting is different. The SCORE model is a great starting point to get the basic meeting objectives right. From there, tailor objectives to suit your specific meeting purpose.

Together, the specific purpose and meeting objectives act as the promo ad for meetings. When considered and defined well, this promo ad will attract invitees to attend. Then, high attendance increases the likelihood of a successful meeting.

In contrast, vague purpose and objectives create a poor, empty promo ad. Imagine you receive a meeting invite like that. Likely, your first response is to decline this invitation because of the lack of information.

Clarity is key to achieving great outcomes. Next, ensure the right people are invited to the meeting.

Action Items

Translate Why to What – Distil key objectives from the meeting purpose

Use the SCORE framework to define meeting objectives:

- *Objective #1: Introduce the current situation and challenges that need to be resolved.*
- *Objective #2: Discuss different opportunities that can address the challenges of the current situation.*
- *Objective #3: Agree on specific next steps to resolve and wrap up the meeting.*

Tailor the objectives based on your meeting purpose.

LESS IS MORE – WHO NEEDS TO BE PRESENT TO ACHIEVE THE MEETING OBJECTIVES

Mariam and I love music. Our favourite way to enjoy music is through live events. It is magical to see artists perform live and experience the rich atmosphere with a big crowd. The Sydney

Symphony Orchestra is a regular for us. Every performance is a wonderful treat to our senses, whether we attend indoor concerts in the beautiful Sydney Opera House or outdoor in a park with a gorgeous backdrop of fireworks.

A symphony orchestra consists of four instrument families: the String family ranges from the smaller violins and violas through to the majestic and massive cellos and basses. Oboes, clarinets, bassoons, and flutes make up the elegant Woodwinds family. The Brass family packs powerful French horns, trumpets, trombones, and tubas. Finally, the Percussion family adds beats and enticing effects to make the rich experience complete.

Each family is relevant. Each instrument has a role to play. Symphony orchestras are well-balanced and sequenced. They avoid unnecessary overwhelming of one instrument family by another. Treat meetings the same way.

Ensure that the right people are invited to deliver the best outcomes.

A frequent complaint about meetings revolves around the guest list. A great meeting brings together a well-balanced group of people who are relevant and add value. Employees are sick and tired of talkfests that fail to achieve positive outcomes.

When investing money, you want to ensure it is invested as best as possible given the circumstances and available information. In a similar way, people invest time and collective thinking and decision-making power in meetings. Ensure that the right people are invited to deliver the best outcomes.

Relevance is the key word. Based on the specific purpose and meeting objectives, identify the right guest list.

Step 1: Relevance is key - Who needs to be there?

Meetings are about progress. The specific purpose and meeting objectives outline the level of desired progress to be made. There are two critical criteria to identify relevant invitees: experts and decision-makers.

For the topic of discussion and objectives, who has relevant knowledge to share and discuss in the meeting? They are the experts.

The term decision-maker means different things to people. Whilst the CEO or department head is a decision-maker, they may not be a relevant decision-maker for your meeting.

Instead, consider the following question: Given the outcomes you want to achieve with your meeting, who is/are the relevant decision-maker(s)?

Step 2: Less is more - Who does not need to be there?

Some people like to invite their entire team to meetings including the most junior support staff. They claim: "everyone needs to be kept in the loop." It is important that people are well-informed about key decisions. However, that does not mean every person should be part of every single meeting. Invite team members only if they have a relevant role during the meeting.

> *Meetings take time, so divide and conquer to invest time wisely.*

Teams have a variety of priorities. Attending a meeting means other work cannot be done in parallel. Meetings take time, so divide and conquer to invest time wisely. It is possible to update team members afterward and get more work done? Take the first shortlist of invitees and play the devil's advocate. For each person on the list, ask: "does this person really need to attend, or is there something better they can do?"

Smart investment of resources and time is about relevance and priorities. Also, consider that less is more. Every added attendee increases the risk of talkfests and lengthy discussions going back and forth.

As the meeting organiser, you are well placed to determine the right guest list to achieve the meeting outcomes.

ACTION ITEMS

Less is More - Who needs to be present to achieve the meeting objectives

Consider the specific purpose and objectives for your next meeting and answer the following questions to define the right guest list:

1. *Relevance is key – Who needs to be there?*
2. *Less is more – Who does not need to be there?*

Play the devil's advocate and divide and conquer to use time wisely.

IN A NUTSHELL

In this chapter you have learned about the Why, What, and Who. Together, they form the critical building blocks for the Context. To schedule meetings smarter, you need to nail this Context first.

Put these learnings to practice and you will complete the groundwork for an exceptional meeting like a true maestro.

Learning is about practice. Invest time for each meeting to follow the process to obtain clarity of purpose, objectives, and relevant attendees. In the beginning, this will take some time.

But practice makes perfect. Like learning how to ride a bicycle, the more you practice, the quicker you will complete the process over time.

Instead of defaulting to the status quo of organising meetings without careful consideration, you are in pole position to deliver better meetings and better outcomes. Your attendees will thank you for that. Over time, you will reap the benefits of someone who is recognised by your peers as one who prepares and thinks thoroughly through situations and makes progress: a better leader!

In the next chapter, you will learn how to use the context to get the meeting process right.

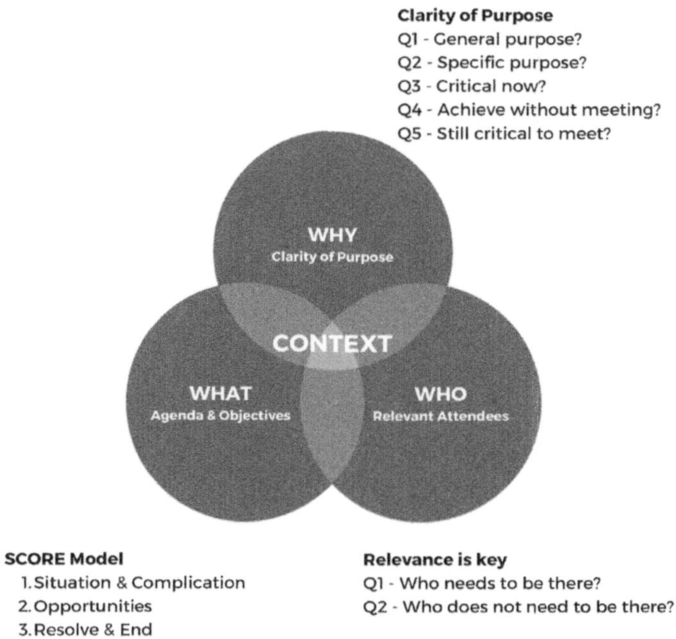

NOTES

1 Stephen R. Covey, The 7 Habits of Highly Effective People (Pocket Books, 2004), 96-99.

2 "Minto Pyramid & SCQA," Model Thinkers, accessed 27 February, 2021, https://modelthinkers.com/mental-model/minto-pyramid-scqa

3 Virgina Satir, James Stachowiak, Harvey A. Taschman, Helping Families to Change (Jason Aronson Inc., 1994), 85-86.

3 GET THE PROCESS RIGHT

ENSURE CLEAR RULES OF ENGAGEMENT

As a kid in the Netherlands, I grew up playing many sports: Hockey, football, and tennis. I loved it all. But when I moved to Australia, I did not have the same habit for a while. I would go for a sporadic run or swim, which I did not enjoy that much.

Then in 2018, I got inspired. Mariam and I love to watch action movies and tv series with heroes who use martial arts to fight off bad guys and save the day. And wow! I found it fascinating to see these different fighting styles and moves. It felt like complete magic to me. It would be amazing to try out.

So, I signed up for a trial class at the International Wing Chun Academy, a short 10 minutes' walk from our home. A few days later, it was time for my trial class. Instructor Stephen welcomed me and explained what was going to happen: the class would start with a warm-up, then segue into practice of specific moves, and conclude with a high-intensity warm-down. He also pointed out instructors, wearing a blue or red sash.

After this comprehensive introduction, I felt well-informed. I knew what to expect and how I could make the most of the trial class. It was clear to me that the team had thought well about how to prepare and run a successful class.

In contrast, I have experienced events that were an unorganised chaos. One time, I attended an event where organisers were busy finishing last-minute details. There was no clear welcome, no instructions of what to do or what would happen when. The entire experience felt like a mess of poor preparation. Some participants left as a result.

Follow the right steps to design a process that feels clear and logical to your participants.

Once you have nailed the context of your meeting, it is time to get the process right. Follow the right steps to design a process that feels clear and logical to your participants, like what I experienced in my trial Wing Chun class.

To get the process right, there are three key areas:

1. **Flow** – What is the right sequence for meeting success?
2. **Etiquette** – What are the rules of engagement?
3. **Roles** – Who is doing what?

Apply these strategies to get the meeting process right from start to finish and achieve your desired outcomes.

FLOW IS EVERYTHING – CREATE A STEP-BY-STEP MEETING SUCCESS RECIPE

In 2012, I discovered Jamie Oliver's *Ministry of Food* cooking book. Before that, I cooked a handful of basic dishes without inspiration. Now, I realised cooking could be easy and enjoyable. The section titles enticed me: 'Twenty-minute meals', "simple soups", "quick-cooking meat and fish", and so forth. I was excited and embarked on a culinary journey of cooking delicious yet simple dishes.

> *Flow is about how to get to your desired result: the specific purpose and objectives.*

Recipes provide a step-by-step approach for transforming ingredients into a delicious meal. What a recipe is to cooking a dish, meeting flow is to delivering great meeting outcomes. Flow is about how to get to your desired result: the specific purpose and objectives.

There are three key considerations for Flow: Activities, Timing, and Review.

Step 1: Activities – What do we need to do and/or share to achieve the outcomes?

It is not enough to know your purpose and objectives. Objectives are not instructions. Flow translates objectives into instructions. Consider this: the goals of cooking are to:

1. Gather and prepare your ingredients.
2. Cook and mix your ingredients.
3. Taste, fine-tune and serve your dish.

I would still be lost with those cooking objectives. Would I need to slice veggies finely or roughly? Boil or fry the meat? Mix everything together or in a specific sequence? And so forth. Each variation changes the outcome.

To translate your context into meeting flow, first write down your specific purpose and three meeting objectives. Then, reflect on this question: "to achieve each objective, what activities do I need to do and/or what content to share?"

The list of possible activities is endless. Each meeting is different, and you can be as creative as you need to be to define the right activities to achieve your outcome.

Objective	Sample Activities
#1 Situation & Complication	• *Do an icebreaker* • *Tell a story* • *Present a case study* • *Show a video* • *Use an infographic*
#2 Opportunities	• *Conduct a Q&A* • *Self-reflection and post it notes* • Pair/small group *brainstorming* • *Whiteboarding* • *Panel discussion*
#3 Resolve & End	• *Majority vote* • *Decision-maker decision* • *Summarise minutes*

Once all ideas are listed, rewrite them in a logical way and remove redundant activities.

Also, consider how you would like participants to feel during the meeting. For example, in late 2019, I delivered multiple team-building workshops for a public sector department. One desired outcome was to facilitate honest conversations about challenges within the team and define improvement initiatives to drive positive change. It does not make sense to start a workshop with these types of discussions. Instead, I built up to these vital conversations by starting with icebreaker exercises and small-group brainstorming discussions. As a result, participants felt comfortable sharing with each other. It became easier to discuss the tough topics and pave the way to tangible, positive progress.

Make the most of the available time, especially when it comes to busy, time-poor senior stakeholders.

Step 2: Timing – What minimum time is needed for each of the agenda items and activities?

When I started to cook more, I learned ingredients have different cooking times to achieve the desired flavours and textures.

The same holds true for meetings. Define a meeting outline that is balanced and flows well. For each activity, consider the ideal timing. If you spend too long on one activity, participant focus may start to falter. Equally, not enough time on a critical activity can lead to poor decisions.

Make the most of the available time, especially when it comes to busy, time-poor senior stakeholders. When unsure, discuss your ideas with an experienced and supportive colleague.

Step 3: Review – Imagine the Flow – What fine-tuning do you need to make it feel right?

Whilst I enjoy cooking, I tend to forget something vital every now and then. Mariam has reminded me many times: 'Don't you taste your own food?' Before serving, taste the food to make sure that flavours are balanced and delicious. Does it have enough taste, is it too sour or sweet, does the dish require any fine-tuning before being served?

Once you have put together your meeting flow with activities and timing, 'taste' your meeting outline by reviewing the flow from start to finish.

I use visualisation and run meeting flow through my mind. I imagine the participants, take them through the kick-off, then transition into the different presentations and exercises. I imagine what the energy will be like and the quality of discussions from beginning to end. Whilst I complete this process, I ask myself:

- Does the overall flow feel right?
- Is anything missing?
- Is anything redundant?
- Do we need to spend more or less time in certain areas?
- Do I need to reshuffle anything?
- Do I feel confident that we can achieve the meeting objectives with the current flow?

I complete this process a few times. The answers to these questions help me fine-tune and streamline the meeting flow until I am confident that it is right.

Action Items

Flow is Everything – Create the step-by-step meeting success recipe

Consider the context for your next meeting and answer the following questions to create your step-by-step meeting outline success recipe:

- *Activities – What do we need to do and/or share to achieve the outcomes?*
- *Timing – What minimum time is needed for each of the agenda items and activities?*
- *Review – What fine-tuning do you need to do make it feel right?*

Use visualisation and review your meeting 'in your mind' until it feels right.

Capture your Meeting Flow in my Meeting Flow Template (see the 'Become a Meetings Maestro today' section at the end of this book with instructions on how to access online bonus resources).

ETIQUETTE – DOS AND DON'TS FOR A SUCCESSFUL CONVERSATION

'How disrespectful!', I thought years ago, as I sat in an important meeting and, suddenly, a cell phone rang next to me. To my surprise, the person answered the call. I assumed he would ask the other person to call back later. However, he continued to talk with the other person in the middle of our meeting. He tried to keep his voice down and whisper. Still, I could not follow the meeting properly anymore. I was getting increasingly annoyed with this disrespectful behaviour.

There is good in digital devices. However, they also increase distractions and reduce presence and focus, especially when it matters most. Successful meetings that achieve outcomes require presence and focus. To plan a productive meeting, rules of engagement matter: the Do's and the Don'ts for a successful conversation. Great problem-solving and decision-making depend on clear communication and focused attention.

People often think that clear etiquette and respectful behaviour is common sense. However, the reality is often different. I have participated in many meetings where participants are glued to their screens and pretend to 'multi-task' by checking emails and other work, despite a presenter's best efforts to keep everyone engaged and involved.

Great problem-solving and decision-making depend on clear communication and focused attention.

You get what you tolerate. Being upfront and clear about desired behaviours – your desired etiquette – in meetings is crucial.

The House of Commons is the primary chamber in the United Kingdom's parliament. I find it fascinating to watch a proceeding of 'The Commons'. Its room in the Palace of Westminster in London is stunning. Long rows of green benches surrounded by rustic wooden walls and window frames with magnificent chandeliers hanging overhead.

Watching a proceeding can be quite confusing. The Commons' debates – with politicians standing up, sitting down, sharing 'hear, hear' – are unique in comparison to other countries. The House of Commons has defined etiquette in remarkable detail. The 'Rules of behaviours and courtesies in the House' document[1] outlines several topics, ranging from requesting to speak, the importance of quickness, how and when to intervene in someone else's speech, through to the correct use of Parliamentary language and properly addressing other politicians present.

Some might say that etiquette and behaviour should not be too tightly regulated, which is a fair point. However, you may recall meetings where rules of engagement were unclear. Disrespectful behaviours make a case for defining some ground rules to maximise successful conduct in meetings.

Etiquette acts as this 'code of conduct' to increase collaboration and productivity of meetings. Consider two key considerations to define the right etiquette for your meeting:

Etiquette Consideration #1 – Presence & Focus

In September 2018, I volunteered at the youth development program 'Green Supercamp Australia' at the stunning Cave Hill Creek near Beaufort, Victoria. The camp helps teenagers develop life and academic skills to improve confidence and success in life. The participants face a big challenge upon arrival: the camp is technology-free. Smart watches, phones, tablets, and laptops – everything is handed over to the crew for safe-keeping. It is a big ask. Today, people use digital devices almost non-stop for work and play. Most of the youth are quietly resigned, some swear and complain loudly.

Etiquette acts as this 'code of conduct' to increase collaboration and productivity of meetings.

However, I love seeing the participants adopt quickly to technology-free environments. They connect and engage more deeply with each other. They learn again how to be curious and ask questions that help them form incredibly inspiring bonds with each other. Some of the most amazing feedback typically comes from those who gave up their devices whilst 'kicking and screaming'; "thank you for taking away my phone, I have made some amazing friends here!"

To achieve meeting objectives, presence, and focus are paramount. For my workshops, I have copied the technology-free experience from the camp. Attendees are not allowed to bring their laptop, and phones need to be switched off. Of course, a gentle reminder may be needed from time to time.

What etiquette do you need to maximise presence and focus?

Etiquette Consideration #2 – Quality of discussion

During my research for this book, I conducted countless interviews with managers. I was eager to obtain insights on the good, bad, and ugly of meetings. A common 'ugly' formed around the quality of discussion. Sometimes, people just interrupt each other without asking for permission to speak. A worse practice is people speaking over the top of others just to get a point through. Interruption, unfortunately, is a poor and frequent practice today, whether in a formal meeting between a board of directors or a casual catch-up between friends.

Being interrupted is often a negative and disempowering experience for people.

Being interrupted is often a negative and disempowering experience for people. Especially when it happens more than once. To foster a positive discussion in meetings, consider what rules of engagement you must establish to make sure all participants can chip in without creating unnecessary tension.

With the COVID-19 pandemic, virtual meetings became a new norm for organisations. In these meetings, it is even more difficult to manage quality of discussion well. Whilst tools like Microsoft Teams have a built-in 'hand-raising' feature to accommodate this, it depends on the meeting organiser to what extent participants use and stick to these features.

Take a moment to review your experience from recent meetings. What was the quality of discussion? Use your learnings as a guide to define what etiquette is needed for future meetings. Clarity is key to help attendees understand the do's and don'ts of proper conduct and achieve meeting outcomes.

What etiquette do you need to put in place to facilitate an empowering discussion?

Every meeting is different. Duration, meeting purpose, participants – each variable plays a role in figuring out what etiquette may be needed. But clarity upfront is key. Without clear etiquette, meetings are left to chance and undesired behaviours may sprout up. Instead, define clear ground rules to set your meeting up for success.

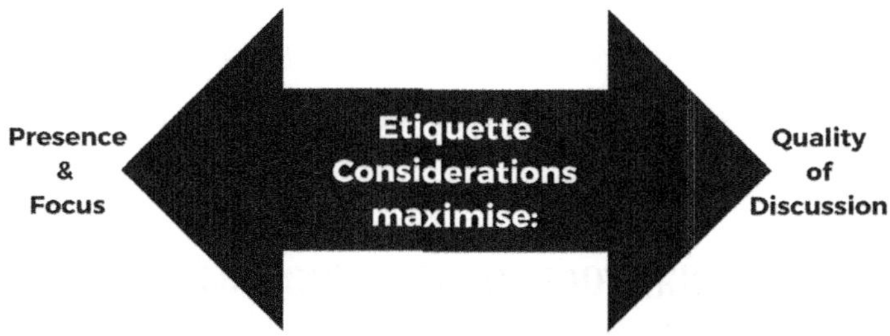

© ST Hoogwout 2021

Action Items

Etiquette – Do's and Don'ts for a successful conversation

Review your most recent meetings and consider what behaviours got in the way of maximising presence and focus as well as quality of discussion.

Reflect and write down your realisations:

What etiquette do you need to put in place to maximise presence and focus as well as nurture the best possible discussion quality?

Write down:

- X *Behaviours and/or things banned in my meeting.*
- ✓ *Behaviours and/or things encouraged in my meeting.*

Clarity is key: ensure to communicate these do's and don'ts to your attendees.

ROLES – ENSURE YOUR INVITEES KNOW WHAT IS EXPECTED FROM THEM

In late 2007, I was standing on field 1 at the Enschede Hockey Club, surrounded by my teammates. We were listening to our pre-game briefing by coach Vreeman

"Okay, ST, listen up", coach Vreeman said, "Your position is left midfielder. When we are in the offense, your role is to use your passing skills to come around our opponents' defenders and put our strikers in great position to score goals. When we are on the defence, I want you to use your speed to come back down and protect our shooting circle."

Coach Vreeman continued his briefing in a similar way. He accentuated each player's focus areas and responsibilities for the game. He also recalled a few distinctions and key players to watch out for in our opponent. Great coaches are like that, and so are great leaders. They provide clarity to their teams and communicate clear expectations. In turn, this helps teams focus and perform to the best of their ability.

As a meeting organiser, you are the leader of your meeting. To achieve the desired outcomes, you also need to define and communicate clear roles and expectations. Imagine a meeting where no one is taking notes on the agreed next steps and decisions. You will be left scrambling to write down actions from memory. Worse, other participants may have a different interpretation of the next steps. The result is a waste of time and opportunity.

To achieve desired outcomes, you need to define and communicate clear roles and expectations.

Clear roles and expectations are crucial. When you know what is expected from you at a meeting, you will find it is easier to look for opportunities to realise those expectations. Attendees are also more likely to show up and add value in the conversation. Quality discussion drives quality outcomes.

In meetings, there are two types of roles you need to consider: 'Cover the Basics' and 'Insights / Value Add' roles.

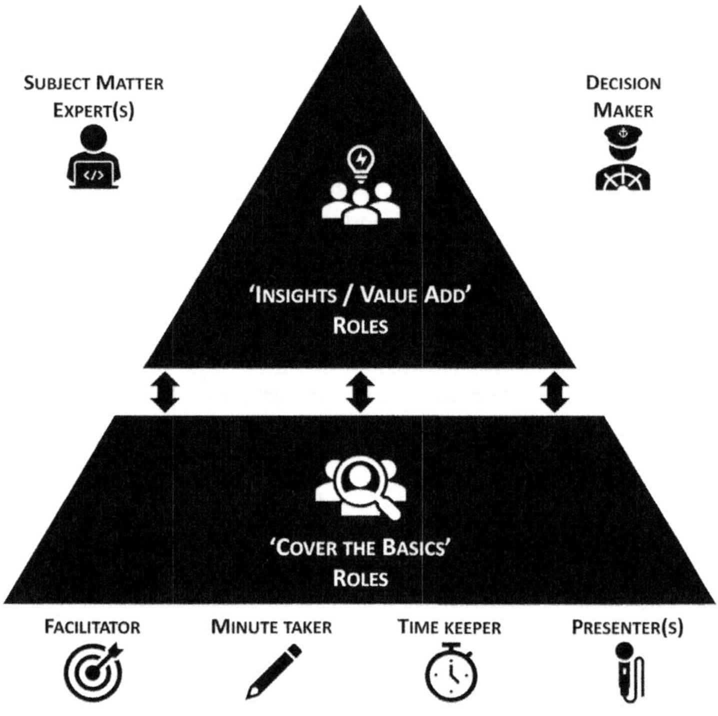

© ST Hoogwout 2021

'Cover the Basics' represent the organisational roles for your meeting. These roles keep the meeting on time and recorded appropriately. 'Insights / Value Add' roles provide the texture and flavour to your meeting. These roles ensure that well-informed decisions are made, considering all the facts and insights needed. Depending on the size of your meeting, certain people may take care of multiple roles.

Role Type	Typical Roles	Responsibilities
'COVER THE BASICS'	Facilitator	Lead the meeting from start to end, navigate the different topics, and manage the overall discussion.
	Minute-Taker	Record decisions and agreed next steps and share with participants to ensure progress is made after the meeting.
	Timekeeper	Keep the meeting on time, notifies the group when specific topics take longer than expected, to wrap up the meeting within the scheduled time.
	Presenter(s)	Present specific topics, share insights on agenda items so that a well-informed discussion can take place.
'INSIGHTS / VALUE ADD'	Subject Matter Expert(s)	Share insights and specialist knowledge to improve problem-solving and decision-making.
	Decision Maker	Owns the topic of discussion, can make decisions and escalate matters when needed, responsible for outcomes.

Ensure participants understand what is expected. Distinguish between general expectations and role-specific expectations. General expectations are things you expect from everyone. Etiquette forms part of the general expectations. But depending on the context, you may expect all participants to come open-minded in case you are looking to obtain new ideas to improve your team structure.

When it comes to role-specific expectations, the starting point is the list of attendees created when you nailed the context of your meeting. Review each person and identify what you expect from them. This is also an important practice to confirm that your meeting is balanced without unnecessary spectators that should be excluded from your guest list. To maximise success, communicate roles and expectations clearly to each participant beforehand. The more specific you can be about what you need from people, especially when it comes to expert knowledge, the better. When you communicate this clearly, people will understand why they are invited and what makes them valuable. This also increases their likelihood to attend your meeting.

Whilst this takes some time, ultimately, this practice delivers successful meetings that save time and achieve exceptional outcomes. Etiquette acts as general expectations for your invitees, while role expectations give attendees clarity about what is expected from them individually.

Action Items

Roles – Ensure your invitees know what is expected from them

Review your list of attendees and consider:

- *What do you expect from each person during the meeting?*

Reflect and write down your realisations.

Distinguish between general expectations (such as etiquette and context-specific expectations) along with role-specific expectations:

- *Who will play 'Cover the Basics' roles of facilitator, timekeeper, minute-taker, presenter(s)?*
- *Who will provide 'Insights / Value Add'?*

Clarity is key: Be sure to communicate these expectations with your participants.

IN A NUTSHELL

After you have nailed the context, it is simple to get the process of flow, etiquette, and roles and expectations right. These three steps set you up for increased success, regardless of the type or size of meeting.

Preparation is not about being perfect. It is about increasing the likelihood for an exceptional meeting that delivers outcomes. Remember, use this level of preparation to consider time and resources well. By doing so, all participants feel that meeting time was well spent and productive.

Now, you are ready to learn the last step to schedule meetings smarter. In the next chapter, you will learn the nuts and bolts of the final details that can still make or break your meeting. To become a Meetings Maestro, you need to be on top of every little thing.

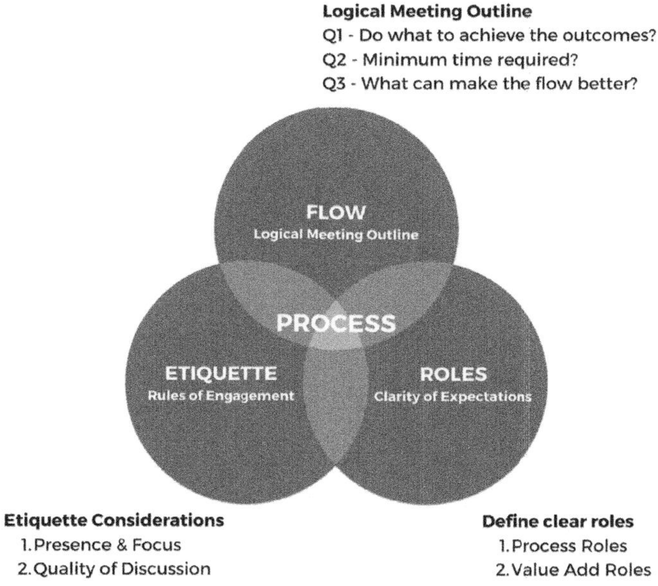

NOTES

1 "Rules of behaviour and courtesies in the House," House of Commons, UK Parliament, last modified December 2015, https://www.parliament.uk/globalassets/documents/rules-of-behaviour.pdf

4 THE DEVILISH DETAILS

THE 3 LAST STEPS BEFORE SENDING YOUR MEETING INVITE

"Drrrrrrrroom, drrrrrrrroom", it sounded, repeatedly. It was late 2020 and my friend, Steve, was in a meeting with a financial advisor in Sydney. Seated in a board room, Steve was excited to discuss different wealth strategies. Everything was on track for a productive conversion. But after a few minutes, deafening drilling sounds came growling from next door: "Drrrrrrrroom, drrrrrrrroom!" "Sorry about that," Steve's advisor said, "they are constructing a new building next door and working on the foundation. Hopefully, it will be over soon."

Steve described this story to me afterward. Still frustrated from the experience, he shared it was one of the worst meetings in his life.

The context for the meeting was spot-on with clarity of why, what, and who. The process was carefully considered beforehand: flow, etiquette, and roles. Despite a solid context and process foundation, the meeting was still a failure.

The final details make a meeting or break it, like in Steve's story. Do not neglect them. Now that you have nailed the context and got the process right for your meeting, the devil is in the detail. Prepare the final three steps before sending out the meeting invite:

1. **Where**
2. **When**
3. **Pre-reads**

Once completed, your meeting is set up for success.

WHERE – IDENTIFY THE BEST SETTING TO ACHIEVE THE MEETING PURPOSE

Location, location, location! Setting matters. Music performances are a fitting example of this. When I was a teenager, I played the trumpet in a fanfare band. Our band specialised in playing famous songs from different decades. Imagine listening to brass versions of your favourite disco, rock, and pop tunes. We would practice together every Sunday night in a plain meeting room. Great for practice, but unfit for a high energy performance in front of an electrifying audience.

Dutch carnival was our busiest and most exciting season. Each year, from the 11th of November, weekly events occur until the five-day Carnival Festival in February. For five days straight, from early mornings to late nights, we would conduct countless performances at a range of different venues. We played outside at street parades and parks and inside at pubs, music halls, and even in the church for the annual carnival's Mass. Tiring, but so much fun!

Setting matters. Each venue has different acoustics and atmosphere. What worked in a pub would not work in the church and vice versa. I am glad we had a great band leader, Anke. Before each performance, she would select fitting songs from our repertoire to match the location and create a unique concert.

To conduct an engaging, purposeful, and effective meeting, identify the best setting that fits the purpose.

Settings matters in music performances, but also in meetings. To conduct an engaging, purposeful, and effective meeting, identify the best setting that fits the purpose of each meeting. Keep in mind that context and process differ for each meeting. Equally, the most proper setting will be different from meeting to meeting too. Rely on your preparation to define the best setting.

Step 1: Given your context and process, what is the best setting: Virtual vs. Face-to-face?

For decades, organisations and employees have been hardwired in a single setting of work. Same location, same office. Then, globalisation increased toward the end of the 20th century. Large corporations set up offices and factories across various locations and geographies to accommodate their market. The use of phone calls and online meetings supports communication between separate locations. Most meetings continued to take place in-person for teams working in the same location.

A major shift in working occurred early in 2020. The coronavirus (COVID-19) went viral and became a pandemic. Organisations asked employees to work from home and stay safe. Instead of meeting in-person, employees would connect remotely via online phone or video calls (also known as virtual meetings).

At the time of writing this book early in 2021, most Australian organisations have embraced a hybrid work model where employees split their work week between office and home. This means that meetings can be held either virtually or in-person. Which is best depends on the context and meeting purpose.

General Purpose	When virtual works better	When in-person works better
RULE OF THUMB	• Bulk of invitees in separate locations • Uncontroversial discussion topic • Small groups (unless to Inform)	• Bulk of invitees work in same office • Contentious discussion topic • Larger groups (unless to inform)
INFORM	• Limited Q&A/discussion anticipated • Uncontroversial topic • Larger groups (5 people or more)	• Substantial Q&A/discussion anticipated • Contentious/difficult topic • Small groups (2-4 people)
IMPROVE	• Tech enables breakouts & idea sharing • Small groups (2-4 people) • Planning and/or brainstorming	• Larger groups (5 people or more) • Team & relationship building focus • Resolving issues and/or performance
DECIDE	• Small groups (2-4 people) • Clear definition of alternatives • Strong participant relationships	• Larger groups (5 people or more) • Ambiguous definition of alternatives • Average participant relationships
PERSUADE	• Strong participant relationships • Uncontroversial topic • Topic well understood	• Average participant relationships • Contentious discussion topic • Topic new / poorly understood

WHERE	Advantages	Disadvantages
In-person / Face-to-face	• Enables better focus & engagement • Allows reading of full body language • Improves connection & relationships • Suited best for difficult conversations	• Time investment (travel / small talk) • Meeting room availability • Least cost effective • Logistics / setup constraints
Virtual (Face-to-face)	• Allows reading of facial expressions • Minimal disruptions to attend • Effective for multiple locations • Ability to record meetings	• Ineffective on a larger scale • Sidebar interactions are difficult • Reduced flexibility for exercises • Requires quality tech and connection
Virtual (Voice only)	• Shorter sessions • Minimal scheduling needs (ad hoc) • Reduced expenses	• Audio only • Ineffective beyond 3 participants • Talking over each other • Poor for difficult conversations

It is possible to conduct a hybrid meeting: Some participants join online whilst others attend in the room. In my experience, it is difficult for online participants to participate in these partial in-person meetings. To make this work, you need to check-in often with online participants to ensure they can contribute and feel part of an inclusive meeting. Ideally, all participants attend either online or in-person, even if some of the participants could meet in a room together.

Given the meeting context and process, should your meeting be virtual or in-person?

Step 2: Use your meeting flow to decide what features or logistics you need

Imagine you have set up the perfect session with your attendees. You kicked off the meeting well, progressing swiftly through the first agenda items. The next item on your agenda is to brainstorm potential improvement initiatives. However, there is a problem. Your plan was to capture ideas on the whiteboard, but all markers are out of ink. 'No problem', you think, and you run to the closest meeting room to grab new markers. The room has another meeting in progress, and you end up disturbing two meetings: theirs and yours.

This happened to me early in my career. The stress and disruptions were unnecessary. I could have prevented this with proper preparation of the setting.

Setting includes more than just location. Items needed for meeting success play a role too. The next step to identify the best setting is to consider these required features or logistics. Meeting flow is your checklist to help you find a suitable setting. Each agenda item or exercise in your meeting flow points to what you might need in your setting.

Review your meeting flow and define the best setting in terms of logistics and features.

If held in-person, a brainstorm session requires a whiteboard, markers, and possibly post-it notes and pens. A team-building session requires space for participants to roam around in pairs or small groups. A status update requires technology for sharing materials on a screen. And so forth.

Equally, online meetings have specific requirements. Do you need a tool that can show videos with sound, facilitate breakout sessions, or conduct anonymous polling? Also, ensure that participants have the right hardware and software to join meetings without any hiccups.

Review your meeting flow and define the best setting in terms of logistics and features. Use the checklist below to consider what elements can improve the end-to-end meeting setting.

WHERE	In-person Room	On-line Meeting
Room Considerations	• Whiteboard? • Flipcharts? • Projector + screen? • Chair/table setup?	• Breakout rooms? • Shared whiteboard? • Polling/voting? • Participant hardware/software prerequisites?
Exercise Supplies	• Coloured whiteboard markers? • Post-its + pens? • Notebooks / sheets of paper? • Specific exercise requirements?	• Coloured whiteboard markers? • Post-its + pens? • Notebooks / sheets of paper? • Specific exercise requirements?
Energy Boosters	• Charged bluetooth speaker? • Charged phone & playlists setup? • Charged laptop? • Presentation / video materials?	• Music/video playback? • Webcams? • Ability to stand/sit easily?

Given the meeting context and process, what is the best setting?

Step 3: Review what else can improve your meeting

Your answers to question 1 and 2 form the criteria for your ideal meeting setting. Before you move on, pause, and reflect:

What are other important considerations to keep in mind?

Ensure that you define the best possible setting. For example, there is value in meeting outside of your regular office for an in-person, team-building session. For a brainstorm session, a bright meeting room with an abundance of natural light can stimulate expansive thinking. Personally, I play relaxed feel-good music during my workshop exercises.

Features change the experience. So, take time to refine your criteria. Then, you can find a fitting setting that evokes the desired frame of mind in your participants.

Step 4: Narrow in on the best setting

Great work! Now, you have solid criteria to pick the best setting. Use this to pick the right technology tool for a virtual meeting or select the best meeting location for an in-person meeting.

ACTION ITEMS

Where – Identify the best setting to achieve the meeting purpose

Use your context and process to identify the best setting for your meeting and consider:

1. *Given your context and process, what is the best setting: Virtual vs. Face-to-face?*
2. *Use your meeting flow to decide what features or logistics you need.*
3. *Review what else can improve the quality of your meeting.*
4. *Narrow in on the best setting*

The devil is in the detail; the wrong setting can break your meeting, whilst a great setting maximises meeting success and participant experience.

TIMING IS CRITICAL – DECIDE WHAT'S BEST TO ACHIEVE YOUR OUTCOMES

In spring 2015, I travelled with Mariam to Japan for a two-week holiday. We had an amazing trip overall, but one thing did not go as hoped. Prior to the trip, we had seen amazing photos of majestic cherry blossom trees in Ueno Park, Tokyo. We hoped to catch the view with our own eyes. But when we arrived in Tokyo mid-May, we had missed the best window. There was no blossom left. We were at the right place, but the wrong time.

Proper preparation can help to be at the right place at the right time. The same holds true for meetings. Time plays a role in achieving meeting outcomes. There are better and worse times to consider. To decide the best time for a meeting, there are three considerations: duration, timing, and buffer.

Consideration #1: Duration – Shorter is better

"It is a commonplace observation that work expands so as to fill the time available for its completion", British naval historian and author Cyril Northcote Parkinson wrote this opening line for an essay for The Economist in 1955[1]. The focus of his essay was on the lack of efficiencies in the British Civil Service. But his quote points to a crucial time-management theme: when a deadline is far in the future, people put off work. Similarly, I waited till the last moment to study for my exams or write my assignments.

PARKINSON'S LAW

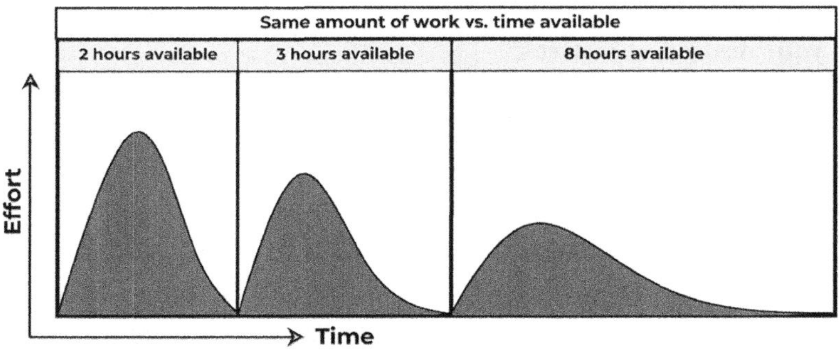

Source: https://www.consuunt.com/parkinsons-law/

As the chart above shows[2], the more time allocated to an outcome, the more time that is used overall, regardless of the number of sub-tasks. The same holds true for meetings. Attendees find ways to fill up the entire meeting time with more discussion.

Challenge the status quo. Online calendars often use default 30- or 60-minute blocks. This does not mean you have to abide by them. Consider your agenda and meeting flow and assess:

what is the minimum required? Get used to scheduling shorter meetings with irregular durations of 10, 20, or 35 minutes.

Shorter is better – take heed of Parkinson's Law to reduce overall time needed and your invitees will thank you for it.

Some people like to chitchat during meetings. But meetings are not for chitchat. Meetings are to make progress. If you feel there is a lack of connection in your team, set up a dedicated team or 1-on-1 session as opposed to using valuable time that was allocated to solve problems.

Online calendars often use default 30- or 60-minute blocks. This does not mean you have to abide by them.

Be critical, what is the minimum time needed to achieve your desired objectives?

Consideration #2: Timing – When is best to get the best energy

I love to facilitate workshops. Workshops are a remarkable journey for teams. People get to know each other better and they design tangible improvement areas together. I love every aspect of it, from preparation through to delivery. It feels wonderful to see real progress. I particularly enjoy seeing the energy between people during my exercises. You can feel how connection and trust blossom. Smiles and laughter are just a fraction of the visible indicators.

In late 2019, I was hired to conduct a culture development program for a public sector department. The client had split up their team of 100 employees into five separate groups. My task was to facilitate discussions around a different topic for each group. The discussions would lead to a prioritised list of culture-improvement initiatives. Overall, the program was a success: participants reflected positively on the sessions, and they had defined valuable improvement initiatives.

Whilst each session had a similar end-to-end flow, I noticed subtle differences in energy levels between each workshop. At first, I attributed this to different participants. But then I realised time differences played a role. Each session was scheduled at a different time in the day. I noticed morning sessions generally had a higher level of energy and engagement compared to sessions held after lunch.

Reflect what level of alertness is critical for your meeting purpose to select an appropriate time.

A 2002 Harvard Medical School study[3], conducted by Kenneth Wright, Joseph Hull and Charles Czeisler, investigated the relationship between alertness, performance, and body temperature in humans. Fourteen adults participated in a 55-day trial in which they were exposed to shifting sleep/awake schedules and exposure to light. On average, the findings highlight that human alertness and performance are at the highest level after waking up and gradually decrease during the day.[4]

These findings align with what I experienced in my workshops. Even though everyone is different and follows their own sleeping routine, timing matters. Reflect what level of alertness is critical for your meeting purpose to select an appropriate time.

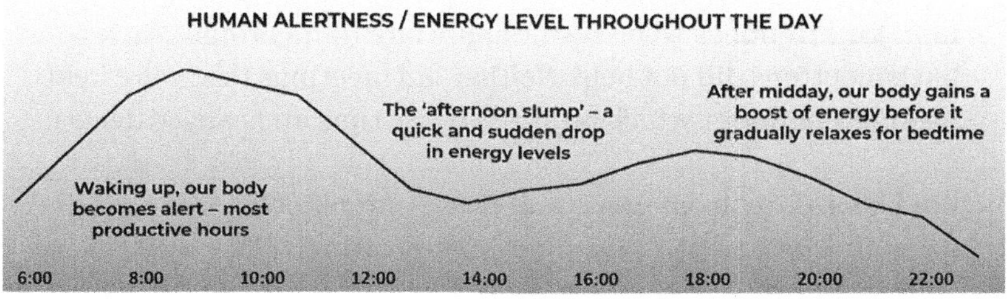

For example, a 1.5-hour workshop requires high energy and engagement; therefore, morning is better. Short and sharp update meetings can be held at any time in the day. Use the energy level chart in combination with your meeting purpose to pick the best time.

Of course, meeting times are subject to other variables. It matters how much time you need to achieve the objectives. It also matters what availability attendees have. Typically, there is more flexibility for non-urgent meetings that can be held in the future than urgent meetings that need to be held as soon as possible.

If you are dealing with one or two participants and multiple meeting timeslots, it is a good idea to ask your invitees when is most convenient to meet. Unfortunately however, this is not often feasible with busy calendars.

Given the level of energy and engagement required for meeting success, what is the best timing?

Consideration #3: Buffer – Account for busy schedules

"You know what", my friend Andrea told me, "I thought that meeting punctuality would have improved with working from home!" It was mid-2020 and she was a managing director at a Sydney-based consulting firm. As a result of the COVID-19 pandemic, entire organisations were now working from home.

Andrea raised a good point. In the old model, it was not uncommon for attendees to be fashionably late to meetings. Back-to-back meetings did not help. Neither did meetings that were held on different floors, which required travel time and caused delays.

But by working from home and using online tools for meetings, it should be easy to join meetings on time. The reality was different. It is frustrating to burn precious meeting time waiting for key participants to arrive. There is a solution. Plan meetings with better timing.

Back-to-back meetings are common for senior executives. In an ideal world, each meeting finishes on time, allowing participants to arrive on-time for their next meeting. But accept it, some meetings go over time. If they do finish on time, back-to-back meetings do not allow for a quick break to reset.

So be smart about it. Use a buffer to account for busy schedules. Do not schedule meetings straight after already scheduled meetings. Instead, include a 5-minute buffer to allow participants to reset, have that toilet break, or grab a quick drink. Your participants will thank you for this time. Instead of waiting in frustration, you can start your session on time with focused attendees.

> *It is frustrating to burn precious meeting time waiting for key participants to arrive. Plan meetings with better timing.*

Whether you need buffer time depends on your audience. If one or multiple busy executives are invited, be safe rather than sorry: schedule that buffer!

Given the audience, how much buffer time is required to hit the ground running from the get-go?

Action Items

Timing is Critical – Decide the best meeting time to achieve your outcomes

For your next meeting, consider your context and process and identify the best time to achieve your outcomes.

1. **Duration** – Shorter is better.
   ➢ *Be critical, what is the minimum time needed to achieve your desired objectives?*
2. **Timing** – Select the best time for the best energy levels.
   ➢ *Given the level of energy and engagement required for meeting success, what is the best timing?*
3. **Buffer** – Account for busy schedules.
   ➢ *Given the audience, how much buffer time is required to hit the ground running from the get-go?*

Poor timing can result in precious time wasted, so be smart about it. Consider your audience and outcomes, use timing as your friend and prepare for meeting success.

SET YOURSELF UP FOR SUCCESS – ARM PARTICIPANTS SO THEY COME WELL-PREPARED

"I am sorry, what is this meeting about?" I cringe on the inside every time someone tells me they were asked that question. I feel bad for them and their audience! It is a missed opportunity when people do not know what they are invited for. Clarity is key and proper preparation prevents similar issues.

Even if you have nailed the context of your meeting and you have gotten the process right, your work may go to waste if invitees feel confused about the purpose of the meeting and do not show up. Meeting organisers hate it when their participants do not prepare or fail to appear. Equally, meeting organisers should make it easy for participants to prepare.

Pre-reads are the information or documents that you send to your audience before a meeting. The purpose of pre-reads is to arm your participants with the right information to come well-prepared. This way, you can make the most of meeting time and achieve the desired outcomes.

The meeting invite is the most important pre-read for your audience

Imagine you are visiting a zoo. You have received a map of the entire zoo, but you have also received separate maps for the reptilian exhibition, aquarium, bird house, and the African wildlife park. Each time you enter a new area, you find yourself searching your map collection to find the right one for where you are now. This is inefficient. It would have been better if there was one map that had little maps on the back to help you find what you are after straight away.

People like things that are easy to understand and follow. Equally, when someone sends you a meeting invite, you don't want to have to do any follow-up work to check what it is about. Instead, at a minimum, the invite holds essential elements such as the meeting purpose, agenda, and objectives, and expectations. If required, you can attach other material for discussion and relevant supporting documents.

PRE-READ ELEMENTS

ESSENTIAL	• Purpose • Agenda & Objectives • Expectations
OPTIONAL	• Materials for discussion • Supporting documents (if any)

When you have nailed the context and process, you have already defined the purpose and objectives (Context) as well as the expectations (Process). Just summarise them into your meeting invite and you are on track. If needed, you can use my meeting invite template:

Meeting Invite Template

Hi everyone,

Key objectives for this meeting are to:

1. ...
2. ...
3. ...

Expectations from you during this meeting are:

1. ...
2. ...
3. ...

Materials for discussion
Attached is a concise x-pager document. For more information about the detail, please refer to slide y.

Let me know in case of any questions beforehand.

I love a special type of pre-read used by the New Zealander trainer Alicia McKay. She works with teams to break down barriers to growth and change. To get her audience quickly in the right frame of mind for her workshops, Alicia records a 3-minute video that explains the agenda, objectives, and key expectations. Video is a great tool to bring people quickly up to speed. Of course, a video is not a suitable pre-read for each meeting, but it highlights how you can use today's technology if desired.

Clean and Clear: Make it digestible, easy to follow

If you do provide more documentation over and above the meeting invite, keep things clean and clear, short, and simple. Nobody likes to spend hours looking for a needle in a haystack, or a piece of analysis that is hidden in a 50-slide document. This book is not about how to write documents clearly but remember to keep any attachments to meetings invites clean and clear. This way, you help your audience to keep things digestible.

But I want to lock in time with attendees before their agendas fill up.

"Hang on ST, I get the importance of doing proper preparation. But I do not want to miss the opportunity of locking in time in calendars of busy people with all this preparation!" Like learning how to ride a bike, the more often you apply these preparation steps, the quicker and better you will become at scheduling your meetings smarter.

Of course, there are instances where you want to lock-in time quickly. In those cases, schedule a quick placeholder and update your invite as soon as possible to provide your invitees with more background. It is worthwhile to note that some people decline placeholders that do not contain other information. Provide attendees with at least 3 days to review pre-reads and arrive prepared to your meeting.

Pre-reads maximise the chance that invitees attend your meeting and know what is expected from them.

Making sure attendees prepare properly

Perfect preparation by you does not guarantee attendees come prepared. Pre-reads maximise the chance that invitees attend your meeting and know what is expected from them.

For certain meetings, you need your attendees to come prepared with questions or insights. Then, you can hit the ground running and make the most of time available. In that case, do not send out information and hope for the best. Instead, do your best to ensure participants do the required work and follow-up. Check in with attendees beforehand once or twice. Remind them of the importance of the meeting and specific expectations you have. Also, follow-up closer to the date and check-in for any questions.

This helps you further streamline your meeting if needed and ensure participants are in the right frame of mind. This extra effort helps you save time by ensuring your audience is ready to go and you do not end up wasting time going through unnecessary background. Also, you might uncover unforeseen conflicts or doubts about meeting urgency, enabling you to address any issues beforehand.

Pre-reads are about maximising meeting success. The better you know your audience, the better you can prepare pre-read materials. Consider their preferred meeting and communication styles. Reflect what you may need to tweak in the meeting materials to keep the conversation at the right level of detail. Any challenges should be thought through to set yourself up for success. If you are not sure, ask your colleagues if they have tips on specific participants so you can use their wisdom for your success.

Action Items

Set yourself up for success - Arm participants so they come well-prepared

Make sure that your audience has clean and clear information about your meeting.

Use the checklist below to evaluate your pre-read materials for your next meeting:

- ✓ *Does your meeting invite contain the essentials: agenda, objectives, and expectations?*
- ✓ *Have you provided presentation and any supporting materials?*
- ✓ *Are the materials clean and clear: digestible and easy to follow?*
- ✓ *Are the materials at the right level of detail for your audience?*
- ✓ *Do you need to follow-up with your audience to ensure they prepare beforehand?*
- ✓ *Have you provided your audience with clear instructions about technology for online meetings (e.g. dial-in details, software requirements etc.)?*

Do not leave things to chance. Do the work and follow-up to maximise success.

IN A NUTSHELL

The final three steps to schedule meetings smarter make an enormous difference.

Imagine receiving a meeting invite that contains clear pre-reads and a considerate setting and timing. Likely, you will feel excited and confident that meeting time will be well spent.

An empty meeting invite is a radical contrast. Why would you click accept an invitation like that?

Proper preparation paves the way to progress. When you apply the final three steps after you have thought through the context and process, your audience will feel the same way. Learning these skills is about improving your ability to think through situations and solve problems. This is a vital leadership skill.

Being able to schedule meetings smarter maximises your ability to conduct meetings well. But more is required to lead meetings that achieve outcomes. In the next section you will learn the six core facilitation skills to become a Meetings Maestro who conducts engaging, purposeful, and effective meetings.

Are you ready? It is time for action and get stuck in delivery!

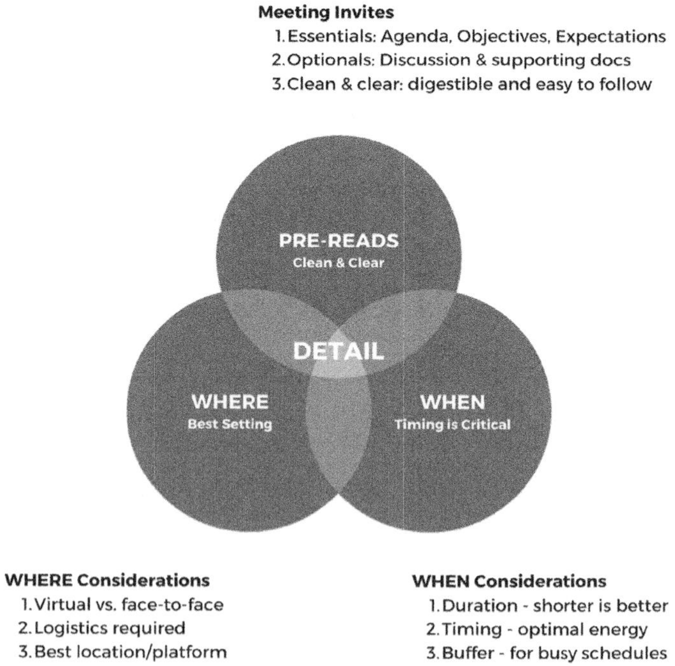

NOTES

1 "Parkinson's Law,", The Economist, accessed 17 March, 2021, https://www.economist.com/news/1955/11/19/parkinsons-law

2 "Parkinson's Law in Time Management", Consuunt, accessed 17 March, 2021, https://www.consuunt.com/parkinsons-law/

3 Kenneth P. Wright, JR., Joseph T. Hull, Charles A. Czeisler, "Relationship between alertness, performance, and body temperature in humans", Harvard Medical School, accessed 20 August, 2021, https://journals.physiology.org/doi/pdf/10.1152/ajpregu.00205.2002

4 "Understanding Your Circadian Rhythm For More Productivity", Self Sector, accessed 21 March, 2021, https://selfsector.com/understanding-your-circadian-rhythm-for-more-productivity/

PART 1 – DESIGN

MEETINGS MAESTRO
SCHEDULE MEETINGS SMARTER

	CONTEXT	PROCESS	DETAILS
PEOPLE	WHO	ROLES	WHEN
FOCUS	WHAT	ETIQUETTE	PRE-READS
ENERGY	WHY	FLOW	WHERE

PART 2 – DELIVER

LEAD MEETINGS THAT ACHIEVE OUTCOMES

5 HIT THE GROUND RUNNING

GRAB ATTENTION FOR A PRODUCTIVE MEETING

In August 2020, Mariam and I moved to a bigger apartment in Sydney. Instead of a single bedroom, we now had two. It was great to use the extra room for my office. Also, the living room was more spacious in comparison to our previous place. Overall, we needed new furniture. I bought a standing desk and highchair from IKEA for my office. We also bought a big buffet table for our living room through eBay.

Our next task was to assemble everything. To our surprise, we loved putting it all together. The IKEA furniture was easy, because of the step-by-step system. The buffet table was a challenge due to vague instructions. But overall, we divided and conquered the process. We enjoyed witnessing how the individual nails, screws, and planks transformed into beautiful, finished products.

Since we loved the assembly process so much, we decided to start puzzling as a hobby. Putting a jigsaw together is a fun little activity. We started with 500-piece landscape puzzles. We then transitioned to more challenging 1,000 and 2,000-piece puzzles. Each puzzle challenged us to refine our strategy and approach. But the start is always the same: finding the outside border and corner pieces.

When the frame is not set, participants can go off-topic and waste valuable time.

The border sets the frame of the puzzle. The same holds true for photos. The frame separates what is in the photo from what is not in the photo. This is also critical for meetings; the frame sets the scene. To hit the ground running, you need to grab attention for a productive meeting and set the right frame and ensure that your invitees are on the same page and interested.

It can be appealing to dive straight into the discussion. But whether your attendees are prepared or not, first spend time to set the frame to focus time and discussion on the right areas without distractions.

When the frame is not set, participants can go off-topic and waste valuable time. Instead, start with a solid foundation for an exceptional meeting that delivers outcomes:

1. Set the scene – recapping the context and process!
2. Elicit buy-in from the get-go.

Transition to each agenda item once the frame is right and everyone is on the same page.

SET THE SCENE – RECAP THE CONTEXT AND PROCESS!

Brrrr, it was so cold. By far, the coldest situation I had encountered in my life. In the summer of 2000, I was on holiday with my family in gorgeous Norway. It was a great trip full of scenic landscapes. One day, we stayed in Hermansverk next to a stunning fjord. Imagine a river of beautifully blue water surrounded by lush green mountains with their peaks covered in blinding white snow. Amazing!

> *Start with a solid foundation for an exceptional meeting that delivers outcomes.*

It was a scorching summer day. After a nice stroll through the town, we were cooling down next to the water and enjoying the views. Close by, locals were enjoying themselves by jumping into the water from a pier. Feeling sweaty, I was tempted to follow their lead. So, I changed into my swimmers and walked to the jumping spot on the pier. Time to go. I ran a few steps and then jumped toward the welcoming water. Instantly, I was out of breath and panting heavily. The water was freezing cold. My body went into direct overdrive to deal with the major temperature drop. I rushed out of the water.

I had forgotten that fjords carry ice water from the mountains. Even in summer, the water does not heat up much despite warm days. The lesson was clear:

Do not jump in cold if you are not ready – ease into it!

Say you have followed the meeting design recipe to the dot. You have nailed the context for your meeting. You got the process right and prepared the final three details before sending out your invite. It can be tempting to jump into the agenda items. However, your participants are not ready to jump in cold.

Maybe they were not able to review your pre-reads due to other priorities. Perhaps your participants were in back-to-back sessions and remain lost in thoughts about a prior meeting. Or challenges at home prevent them from being in the right frame of mind. Whatever the situation is, take a moment to ease participants into the meeting and redirect their focus.

Set the scene by framing the meeting

"Keep an open mind and play along with the different activities. Each activity is designed on-purpose and to help you learn. The more you participate, the more value you will receive." I always share this message at the start of my workshops. It helps people understand that each activity matters. This is important because I use a variety of activities and tools, including some surprises. The message also reminds the audience that their extent of learning depends on how much they participate. It says: if you want value, participate and play along.

When you frame context, you recap the specific purpose of meeting and each of the objectives you wish to achieve through your meeting.

Core Facilitation Skill #1: Framing

Framing is a powerful technique. It provides clarity to your invitees of what to expect and how to behave. After completing the Design process, you have already done the groundwork. Next, use this preparation to frame the context and process.

When you frame context, you recap the specific purpose of meeting and each of the objectives you wish to achieve through your meeting. This is often done naturally by experienced meeting facilitators. Context framing, however, is often overlooked. Process framing provides clarity to attendees about the etiquette, roles, and expectations.

Often, process is left to chance. People assume everyone knows how to behave and what is expected. "To assume, is to make an ass out of you and me (ass-u-me)," I once read. Assumptions can stop progress. Instead, communicate and reiterate clear etiquette and expectations upfront. Make it explicit what behaviours are encouraged and how each attendee can chip in and add value.

Once the table is set, elicit buy-in from the get-go from your audience before moving on.

Action Items

Set the Scene – Recap the context and process!

Do not jump in cold; instead, ease your participants into each meeting.

Practice Core Facilitation Skill #1: Framing:

Clarify to your audience what to expect and how to behave.

At the start of your meeting:

1. *Frame Context* – Remind invitees of the purpose (why), objectives (what) and agenda for the meeting.
2. *Frame Process* – Specify etiquette and expectations from your audience.

Clarity is key for an exceptional meeting that achieves outcomes.

ELICIT BUY-IN FROM THE GET-GO

First impressions count. According to Princeton University researchers Janine Willis and Alexander Todorov[1], it only takes a split second to form an opinion about someone: Do we like someone or not? A sense of trustworthiness and likeability and a few other factors play a role into forming that first, unconscious assessment. From that point forward, people often interact based on that sticky first impression.

Similarly, make the first impression of your meeting count and maximise the probability of meeting success. There are two key elements to hit the ground running and achieve that strong opening.

Imagine, you have framed your meeting well. However, participants are not bought in. Maybe they do not agree with an agenda item or expectation. By rushing to the next item on your agenda, you have already lost part of your audience. Then, it is close to impossible to get them back on board.

Instead, obtain permission before moving on.

Core Facilitation Skill #2: Inquiring

When you meet a new person, non-verbal behaviours play a significant role in forming that first impression. In meetings however, what you say and how you say it plays a dominant role in obtaining buy-in. You might be tempted to assess the level of buy-in based on whether your audience nods along or not. However, it is not effective to rely on your own assumptions and interpretation of these little visual cues. Instead, use inquiry to check-in where the audience is.

Once everyone is together, how you start the meeting decides success or failure. If there is no buy-in at the start, there will not be agreement at the end of the meeting. Instead, consult your audience from the start and throughout the meeting. Then, you work together to define win-win solutions and next steps.

Use effective, open-ended questions to assess and obtain buy-in from the start.

AREA	Obtain Buy-In Sample Questions
CONTEXT	• *What else is important to discuss or achieve in this meeting?* • *What is not important to discuss today?* • *What agenda item(s) do you (not) agree with?*
PROCESS	• *What other etiquette / ground rules should we put in place?* • *What expectations do you have for me?* • *What (other) roles should we put in place?*

Meetings prosper when there is buy-in and engagement. Participants share ideas, add value, and work together to define win-win solutions. Buy-in is required from all participants. Use the check-in questions with your audience and update the context and process based on feedback if needed.

When a meeting is well prepared, the start of a meeting can be short and focused. Then, transition straight into the different agenda items. Sometimes, it is possible that discussion around the meeting context becomes the main meeting. For example, attendees question if the topic of discussion is the right problem to solve and discuss. This could be due to poor meeting preparation or for ambiguous or contentious meeting topics. Use the Design-process to ensure your meeting is topical and relevant now.

Action Items

Elicit buy-in from the get-go

Work with your audience and ensure everyone agrees with the meeting context and process.

Practice Core Facilitation Skill #2: Inquiring:

Use questions to check if your audience is on board and ready to move on.

After framing your meeting, use inquiry to check-in with your audience:

- *Use open-ended questions.*
- *Update the context and process based on feedback.*
- *Confirm everyone is on board.*

After your meeting, reflect and write down:

- *Which questions did you find most effective?*
- *What did you learn from inquiring with your audience?*
- *Which questions will you (not) use in the next meeting?*

Meetings are a waste of time unless there is buy-in around context and process from the start.

IN A NUTSHELL

First impressions matter. You have now learned the key steps to hit the ground running and kick-off meetings in the best conceivable way. Instead of rushing to the discussion of agenda items, you have learned how to use the first two core facilitation skills of framing and inquiring to ease into the meeting.

Like learning any new skill, it may take a little while to get used to applying these skills naturally. At first, it may feel awkward to simply reiterate the objectives of a meeting and robotically ask participants if they agree and whether they would like to add anything. It might also feel very foreign to check etiquette beforehand, since this is often not discussed.

But the more you apply framing and inquiring, you will realise that these skills help you maximise meeting success. Buy-in from the start is critical and a Meetings Maestro is in control from start to finish. Now you can get to the meaty part of your meeting where the rubber really hits the road.

In the next chapter you will learn how to read the energy in the room and how to redirect it when needed. These skills help you transition from a successful start to a successful end of your meeting.

NOTES

1 Janine Willis and Alexander Todorov, "First Impressions", Princeton University, accessed on 24 March, 2021, https://web.archive.org/web/20140715094146/http:/psych.princeton.edu/psychology/research/todorov/pdf/Willis%26Todorov-PsychScience.pdf

⑥ MANAGE THE ROOM

DECIDE WHEN/HOW TO QUICKLY SHIFT THE ENERGY

Music always played an important part in my life. In the mid-nineties, my oldest brother Harmen was hired to host weekly shows for the local radio station in my village in the Netherlands. I would always tune in and visit the studio from time to time too. I got hooked on electronic dance music he often played on the show or at home.

When music television channels became more popular, I realised I particularly enjoyed live coverage of music events. At that time, my favourite show was TMF: The DJs. It featured footage from a nightclub with a disk jockey (DJ) playing dance music in front of an excited crowd. I loved it (and still do): awesome music, lights and lasers, and people dancing. So, I vowed to myself that one day, I would become a DJ too.

My dream came true in 2003. I moved across the country to study at the University of Twente and joined a social student club. The club had its own bar where frequent member nights took place each week. Also, members could join several committees to develop new skills. I joined the so-called MuLiCo – the music and light committee. The MuLiCo made parties come to life. Whether to celebrate the club's anniversary, one of the club factions' anniversaries, orientation week events, or any other reason, we would grasp the opportunity and transform our bar into a night club, complete with lights, smoke machine, and DJ-equipment. In the years ahead, I would DJ at countless events.

If you are unable to redirect the energy in a positive way, knowing where you are is not enough.

Music plays a significant role in shaping a great atmosphere. I learned how to read the energy in the room and what to do when the energy dropped. Each event was an amazing experience. In hindsight, my passion for helping teams boost energy and deliver great outcomes in workshops comes from what I learned whilst playing those tunes for a crowd of party people.

Similarly in meetings, it is crucial for you to read the level of energy: Are you in a good place or not? Once you have a correct assessment of the situation, you can consider if you need to step in and how. If you are unable to redirect the energy in a positive way, knowing where you are is not enough.

In this chapter you will learn the key indicators of how to read the room at any moment. You will also learn what tools works best based on where your meeting is. Once participants are back in the right frame of mind, you can continue an exceptional meeting that delivers great outcomes through productive discussion.

MONITOR THE ENERGY – KEEP AN EYE ON PARTICIPANT ENGAGEMENT AND BUY-IN

When I started as a DJ, I focused on playing my favourite music. However, I noticed that the energy in the room was not great. People enjoy a variety of genres and songs. Balance is key for a successful party where most people are having a great night out. With every event, I learned new distinctions that helped to read the energy in a room.

For example, increased busyness meant people were having fun and vice versa. I would also notice the flow of movement. Were people walking towards the dance floor or away from it? Behaviours such as smiling, laughing, sing along and waving arms to the beat highlighted high energy and a great atmosphere. With each new song or genre, any of these indicators could change instantly, so it was important to constantly keep track. Any drop in energy would point to an opportunity to shift things up. These insights also helped me to understand and read meeting energy indicators.

When the energy is not quite right, the quality of discussion is suboptimal and results in poor outcomes.

Managing meetings well is also about managing energy. When the energy is not quite right, the quality of discussion is suboptimal and results in poor outcomes. You need to be able to read energy well to deliver meetings well. If you misread the energy, any action can drop the energy further. People disengage and you miss out on exploring great ideas, considerations, or questions.

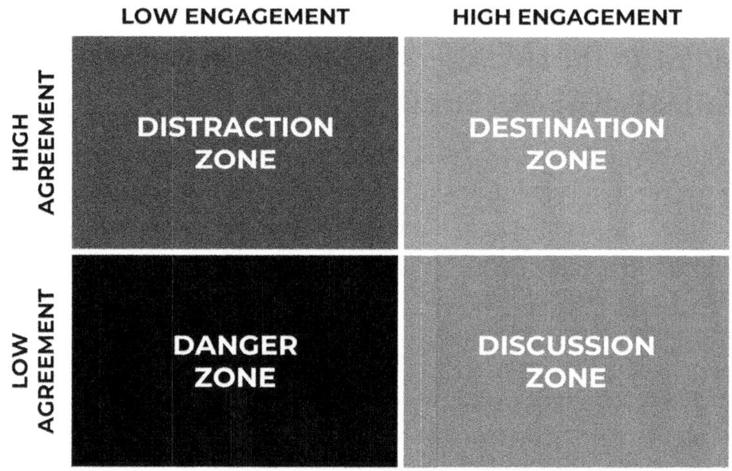

Know Where You Are – The quality of meetings reflects the quality of communication and decision-making in organisations

Imagine you are lost at sea. No matter which way you look, there is endless ocean without any landmarks. How can you find your way if you do not know where you are? In the old days, the position of the sun and stars in the sky formed a clear map. Today, global satellite positioning (GPS) tools provide the right indicators. It is about knowing what to look for.

Core Facilitation Skill #3: Reading the room

In meetings, interactions take many forms. Knowing what to look for to pinpoint the quality of discussion is vital. Once there, your journey toward meeting success can continue.

There are two ingredients to assess the quality of energy in your meetings: engagement and agreement.

Energy Consideration #1: Engagement enhances expertise

When people are engaged, they listen to each other, and they are open to contribute with ideas and insights. The increase in insights helps make better decisions. On the flipside, when there is low engagement, people do not really listen to each other, and they certainly do not add value. Whilst hostility may seem like engagement, it is not constructive in discussing potential solutions and moving forward. High engagement, in a positive and constructive manner, means that the collective expertise of the entire group is used to solve problems together. So, engagement enhances expertise, and ultimately, well-informed decisions and progress.

Engagement enhances expertise, and ultimately, well-informed decisions and progress.

Energy Consideration #2: Agreement accelerates achievement

When you want to go fast, go alone. But if you want to go far, go together. To go together, agreement is required to achieve objectives. Without agreement, progress is blocked. Whilst it may not be possible to always agree on every detail, you need to be able to align on next steps to resolve outstanding issues to further a particular initiative. When meetings fail to achieve alignment among participants, they are a waste of time.

At any given moment, your meeting is in one of four zones based on either low or high engagement and agreement.

Danger Zone – Danger can lead to death

'This is bullshit!', the executive said and stormed out. It was early in my consulting career, and I experienced an extreme situation. A strategy meeting went back and forth between senior executives in an intense argument. They could not agree on anything. Then the 'bullshit' statement came out and the meeting ended abruptly.

Toxic behaviours, such as hostility and avoidance, are indicators of low agreement and low engagement.

Toxic behaviours, such as hostility and avoidance, are indicators of low agreement and low engagement. The danger zone can lead to death: a premature death of your meeting, your project, or worse, your role. In the Danger Zone, meetings fail to deliver results and create team tension that requires time and effort to soften up.

Distraction Zone – Hey, are you with me?

I would be rich if I got a dollar each time an attendee was on a laptop during a meeting. Unfortunately, participants attend in-person meetings with a digital device in many organisations. Common excuses include "I am taking notes" or "I am sending a quick email". In either case, these devices distract people. They send the signal: this meeting is not as important as what I am doing on my laptop. In a virtual meeting, this is more difficult to monitor and regulate as devices are needed to attend in the first place.

Whilst participants might nod along whilst 'multi-tasking', they are not present, and meeting quality suffers. You may consider that nodding along means a high degree of agreement and buy-in. However, do not be fooled. Unfocused buy-in is a problem. When people are distracted and seemingly agree in the moment, they can come back to disagree at a later stage. Presence and focus are vital for high-quality discussion and agreed outcomes.

Discussion Zone – Sharpen solutions based on different views

"I do not agree with that, and here is why." Disagreement is not a bad thing. In fact, constructive disagreement can sharpen problem-solving and outcomes. How different perspectives are shared and discussed matters. Imagine a situation in which a facilitator asks each participant to share their views. Exploring different views with inspired, engaged colleagues is why meetings take place. The Discussion Zone is about positive and constructive disagreement. Contrast this with the Danger Zone of hostile disagreement and avoidance.

Once all views have been explored in the Discussion Zone, it is time to define win-win solutions that make sense for your team

Once all views have been explored in the Discussion Zone, it is time to define win-win solutions that make sense for your team and progress to the:

Destination Zone – What are our agreed next steps?

"Great things in business are never done by one person. They are done by a team of people." Steve Jobs, American business leader and founder of tech company Apple, had it right with this quote[1]. Teams can only achieve remarkable things when they agree to win-win solutions and specific next steps to act upon. For each agenda item and at the end of a meeting, you want to find your meeting in the Destination Zone. Think of it as the end zone in rugby. This is where you want to be. There is high agreement and high engagement about where to move forward.

Rome was not built in one day. So, remember that the Destination Zone is not about agreeing on every single element for a long-term project or strategy. Instead, it is about being on the same page with your attendees about what to do next to further your project right now.

At any given moment, your meeting is in one of these four zones. Your first job is to know where you are. Know what to look for and consider the tell-tale signs and indicators for each zone. The more you practice 'reading' the energy of your meeting, the better you will become at instantly assessing where you are.

© ST Hoogwout 2021

Once you can pinpoint the correct zone, you can redirect your meeting toward the Discussion and Destination Zones when needed.

Action Items

Monitor the Energy - Keep an eye on participant engagement and buy-in

To lead meetings that deliver outcomes, you need to be able to read the energy in the room well.

Practice Core Facilitation Skill #3: Reading the room:

Know in which of the four engagement – agreement zones your meeting occupies at any given time.

During any meeting you attend, check-in:

- *What energy indicators can you observe from the participants?*
- *Based on these indicators, in which zone is the meeting now?*
- *Are specific participants in different zones based on different energy indicators they show?*
- *What else can you observe?*

Keep track of the tell-tale signs of each zone and improve your ability to read the energy well.

JUMP IN PROMPTLY – TACTICS FOR ELEVATING THE ENERGY IN THE ROOM

In my DJ days, I learned so much about people and energy. When I noticed that the energy on the dance floor dropped, I had several tools at my disposal to change gears. It took time to discover which tool worked best. For example, a shift in song or music genre would create a shift in energy. But a radical shift could be off-putting to the people who were still enjoying the music. It matters in which way a shift was made. An abrupt stop and start would cause confusion. Instead, gently fading one song out and another song in would be more appropriate. The best transition was to create a seamless transition by mixing in the new song.

Elements like timing, the choice of genres, different energy levels of each song play a significant role. I discovered what songs worked regardless of the time and what songs or genres only worked at the beginning or toward the end of the night. I learned how to use genre blocks of four to five songs before shifting to a different genre and keeping everyone engaged. I learned the importance of building up energy within a genre block and so forth.

Each tool results in a different type of outcome. Some work better than others. The same is the case in meetings. Despite applying the core facilitation skills of framing and inquiring, it is still possible that a meeting drifts into unwanted territory. Your first task is to know in which engagement-agreement zone your meeting is in. Next, it is time to use the right tool to shift the energy when needed.

When things go off track, you need to reel your audience back in. Knowing when and how to jump in is vital.

Mahatma Gandhi, the Indian lawyer and political ethicist who led the non-violent resistance campaign to achieve India's independence from British rule, did not start his career with remarkable success. In his first case as a lawyer, he was defending someone in the Bombay Small Causes Court. When it was his turn to speak and cross-examine a witness, Gandhi's mind went blank. He was unable to think of any questions or statements. Being unable to represent the case, he withdrew and rushed out.

When things go off track, you need to reel your audience back in. Knowing when and how to jump in is vital. If not, the meeting fails to deliver the intended outcomes. Everyone's time is wasted. Like an effective Chief Executive Officer (CEO) can steer an organisation, meetings require a skilful facilitator to redirect the energy and focus when things do go astray.

Core Facilitation Skill #4: Shifting the Energy

"Hey Robert, could you please shut down your laptop and focus on our meeting?" In early 2016, I was attending a strategy workshop for a financial services organisation in Sydney. The facilitator had laid out some ground rules at the start of the meeting. One request was for participants to keep focused and not use their digital devices. As time went by, some participants got lost in their devices. At one point, the facilitator got fed up and made Robert an example.

Now I can't talk for Robert, but I imagine he felt upset by being put in the spotlight in front of everyone. He obeyed the request. However, he did not contribute anything in the rest of the meeting.

Shifting energy is tricky. When done well, elegant shifts improve the atmosphere in the room. Messy shifts, on the other hand, deteriorate energy. Messy shifts can get the job done. However, they are forceful. Like in the example with Robert, messy shifts create friction and resistance with attendees. Similarly, in classrooms, teachers often call on sleepy or distracted students. This is also messy. The person's response might be to acknowledge they were not paying attention, or they may make up an answer on the spot. Either response is not helpful. It creates unnecessary disturbance and sends the wrong signal to the audience. It is not about enforcing full presence and focus.

> *Elegant shifts are subtle. They get the job done without creating any unnecessary tension.*

Instead, elegant shifts are subtle. They get the job done without creating any unnecessary tension. In other words, elegant shifts drive inclusion and connection across the team, which is always preferred. So, how you shift focus is what matters.

There are three elements you can shift: position, activity, and focus.

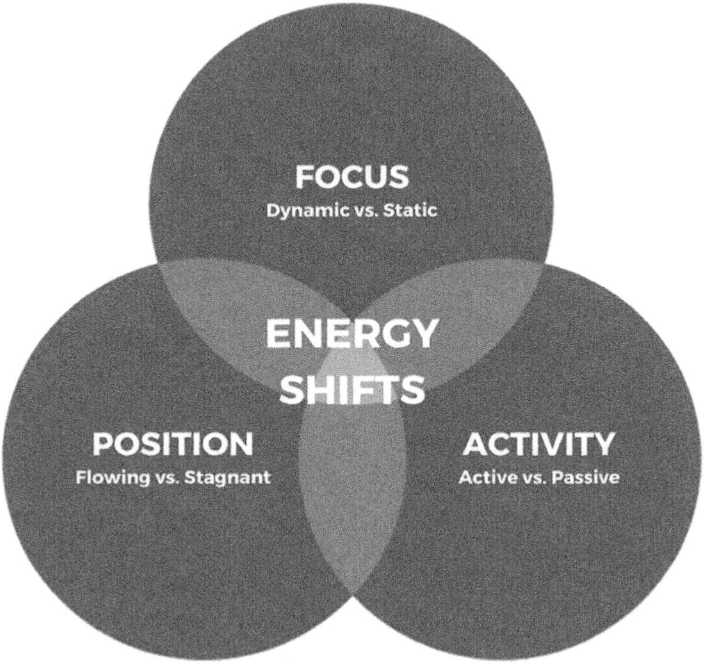

© ST Hoogwout 2021

Position shifts depend on how we use our body. Most participants sit through meetings. However, sitting for too long reduces the energy. A stand-up or a walking meeting have a radically different energy. When needed, switch position by asking participants to stand up or move through the room.

Meetings contain different activities undertaken by the audience. For example, when there is a presenter, participants are listening. But the meeting agenda should include a dynamic range of passive and active activities. In other words, listening is one mode, but sharing ideas and problem solving is more active participation.

Focus is about what participants direct their brainpower towards. Is the presentation about problems, solutions, or next steps? A dynamic focus varies between different elements over time. A static or passive focus is when the meeting is stuck on one person sharing ideas, or only problems being discussed.

To keep the audience engaged, skilful facilitators create energy shifts by changing at least one of these elements, and ideally two or more elements. Matt Church, co-founder of the Thought Leaders Business School, suggests splitting meetings and workshops into five-minute segments. The segments should have a different energy and focus for the audience to keep engagement high. In other words, do something different often to keep interest.

Be gentle, as opposed to messy, for a natural segue. This way, you nurture positive energy and an inclusive group.

So, a brief recess may be beneficial in a long meeting. Participants can move around. Also, they are free to focus on their distractions before returning to a focused discussion. If time is sparse however, a dynamic exercise is the solution. For example, request people to have a sidebar conversation with the person next to them. Instead of listening to the presenter, the audience is now actively participating and sharing ideas. Asking them to stand up and discuss ideas whilst walking around injects fresh energy into the room. That jolt may just inspire novel ideas and create remarkable results.

Whatever you do, change position, activity, and focus to create dynamic and lasting energy shifts. The how matters. Be gentle, as opposed to messy, for a natural segue. This way, you nurture positive energy and an inclusive group.

So as an example, instead of calling out Robert in front of everyone, a more effective solution would be to ask the participants to have a quick discussion in pairs with their neighbour and report back any findings after a few minutes. This boosts engagement without unnecessary friction.

AREA	Active - Examples	Passive - Examples
POSITION *How is our body positioned?*	• Move	• Sit • Stand • Lay
ACTIVITY *What are we doing?*	• Share • Present • Discuss • Write / draw	• Listen • Watch • Read • Process / Think
FOCUS *What are we thinking about or focused on?*	• Switching between topics (e.g. from problems to solutions to next steps) • Switching discussion type (e.g. listen to one person, discussion in pairs/small groups, panel discussion)	• Stuck on a single topic (e.g. just problems, or just solutions) • Single person talking

THE FOUR SHIFTS YOU NEED TO MASTER!

Shift #1: From the Distraction to the Discussion zone

Human beings have a short attention span. A recent study conducted by American researcher Neil Bradbury of the Chicago Medical School indicates that humans do not have a fixed attention span, so it is vital that meetings engage participants to maximise effectiveness.[2] Long meetings increase the chance that attendees get distracted eventually. Our notification-rich devices do not make things easier. Use the Design-process to prepare a dynamic meeting that offers variety in terms of exercises and communication modes to keep things interesting. Listening to one single person talk for over 10 minutes without any interaction is boring. A disconnected audience is inevitable.

Even with the best meeting flow and etiquette, attendees will struggle to remain present throughout. A brief distraction is not an issue. However, when someone stays distracted and others follow suit, it is time to act.

It is not a surprise that presenters themselves are engaged. They are busy sharing information. It takes awareness to assess what the audience might be feeling throughout. A distracted audience is not a bad thing. Instead, perceive these moments as a wake-up call. They are a reminder that meetings should be dynamic and engaging. A disconnected audience means it is time to shift things up. Despite other plans on your meeting flow, be flexible. Instead, recognise when your participants are stuck in passive energy and need a shake-up. Then, use one or a combination of the three 'energy shifts' —position, activity, and focus — to your advantage and reel participants back in without putting individuals on the spot.

A disconnected audience means it is time to shift things up. Despite other plans on your meeting flow, be flexible.

Direct attendees to contribute actively (through position, activity, and/or focus)

Shift 2 – From the Danger to the Discussion Zone

Resistance is what underpins the Danger Zone. Resistance stems from not feeling listened to, understood, or valued. Resistance can either be passive or active. Participants with passive resistance do not contribute. To deal with passive resistance, follow a similar approach to dealing with the Distraction Zone. It is not a guaranteed recipe for success; however, participants will start to share concerns. From there, you can explore ways forward with the group in the Discussion Zone.

Dealing with active resistance is tricky. A person might either be hostile and defensive to an entire group. They could also try to lobby specific people to join them in their thinking. Remember where resistance originates. People resist when they feel ignored and undervalued. In the words of Stephen Covey, 'seek first to understand'[3]. Use your skill of inquiry. Ask people to share their concerns. Listen for what they are saying and follow-up to make sure you are on the same page. Look for common ground in what they share and then re-direct by asking them for solutions given their experience.

Resistance is what underpins the Danger Zone. Resistance stems from not feeling listened to, understood, or valued.

I like the quote, 'if you are not part of the solution, you are part of the problem'. If someone is sharing resistance in an unproductive manner, help them to become part of a win-win solution that matters to them. Your choice of language plays a key role. Use their words and acknowledge their insights as you steer towards solution-oriented thinking. For example, use this line: "I understand your concerns and clearly this is important to you, and you have given this much thought. Given your experience in this matter, I would love to hear your thoughts on a solution that would help create the desired outcomes?"

Seek first to understand and connect before rushing to overcome resistance by force. In some instances, you may need to deal with resistance after a meeting due to time restrictions. However, the same approach will apply to deal with resistance.

Upfront effective icebreakers can reduce resistance. For example, at the start of my workshops, I love to conduct a brief introduction activity that gets people to share and learn about each other. Then, I transition to a 'worry'-exercise that allows people to share their worries with each other. As they listen to each other, they recognise they are not alone in their concerns. This creates both team bonding and the need to explore new opportunities to address issues.

Seek first to understand; find common ground and connect; then re-direct to solution-oriented thinking.

Shift 3 – From the Discussion to the Destination Zone

The shift from Discussion to Destination is critical. You need be able to finish each agenda item by agreeing on specific next steps and ownership. If not, the meeting was a waste of time. It is possible you are unable to agree on every single issue with your participants. But, at minimum, you need to be able to agree on specific next steps to resolve those issues in the future. If handled poorly, you might slide back to the Danger Zone.

You need be able to finish each agenda item by agreeing on specific next steps and ownership.

Use questions to move to the Destination Zone. Key questions to ask are:

- What can we agree upon?
- What do we not (yet) agree upon?
- What are suitable next steps we all feel comfortable with?
- What are suitable next steps considering the objectives we all agreed upon?

Make sure you check to be sure that everyone is on board. In the next chapter, you will learn the specific process to finish your meeting on a high in the Destination Zone.

Seek consensus on next steps and ownership to progress the project or resolve the issue.

Shift 4 – From Destination to the Discussion Zone

Sometimes, you arrive in the Destination Zone quickly. It is great to have high agreement and engagement. You might be tempted to move to the next item on the agenda or close the meeting. However, it is possible that things are left unsaid.

In her book, *Dare to Lead*[4], American research professor Dr. Brené Brown shares two major problems when it comes to meetings: the 'halo effect' and 'bandwagon effect'. The halo effect is a tendency for participants to agree with the most influential person in the room. The bandwagon effect is a tendency for attendees to agree with the majority even though they do not agree. Brown applies the 'turn and learn' exercise to deal with both issues. Before any perspectives are shared, participants are asked to write down what they really think about an issue on a post-it note. Then, everyone is asked to reveal answers at the same time. So instead of hiding, each person must share their real thoughts.

Other organisations use a 'devil's advocate role' and assign it to a specific meeting attendee. The role of that person is to argue against the consensus of a group. The objective is to consider all foreseeable risks and strengthen decision-making.

Alternatively, you can ask your invitees: "if there was anything unsaid, or a potential concern, what would it be?" This way, all participants play a vital role in strengthening problem-solving rather than depending on a single person.

These practices are not about dragging out a discussion unnecessarily. The purpose is to strengthen decisions and consider all variables at stake.

Ask: if you/I did have a concern about this decision, what would it be?

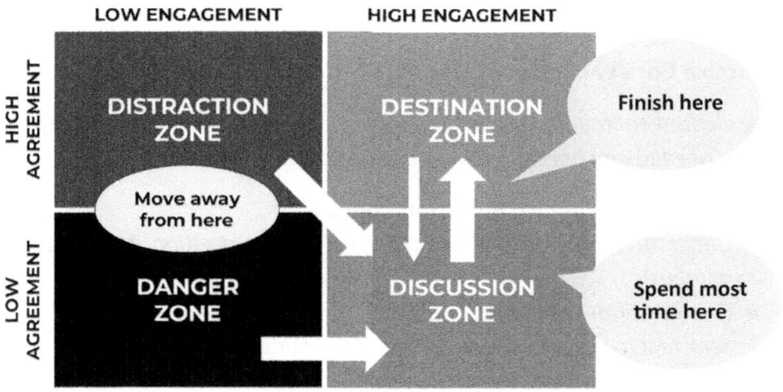

© ST Hoogwout 2020

One final note when it comes to energy shifts and facilitation. Confidence matters. As a facilitator, you are the conductor. Be assertive when directing others to engage in exercises and discussion. Confidence comes from experience. Experience comes from practice. So, use every opportunity to apply your learnings and grow your confidence.

Action Items

Jump in Promptly - Tactics for elevating the energy in the room

Once you know in which engagement – agreement zone your meeting is in, you need to be able to shift the energy in the room when needed.

Practice Core Facilitation Skill #4: Shifting the energy:

Use elegant energy shifts (position, activity, focus) to redirect the energy when needed and finish meetings in the Destination Zone.

- From Distraction to Discussion Zone:
  Direct attendees to contribute actively (through position, activity and/or focus).
- From Danger to Discussion Zone:
  Seek first to understand; find common ground and connect; then re-direct to solution-oriented thinking.
- From Destination to Discussion Zone:
  Ask: if you did have a concern about this decision, what would it be?
- From Discussion to Destination Zone:
  Seek consensus on next steps and ownership to progress the project or resolve the issue.

After your meeting, reflect and consider:

- What type of energy shifts did you apply for each shift?
- What worked well?
- What did not work well?
- What did you learn for next time?

Practice makes perfect; experiment with different shifts and evaluate which work best for you to shift the energy and lead meetings that achieve outcomes.

IN A NUTSHELL

Your ability to read meetings well and shift the energy is what separates poor meetings from engaging, purposeful, and effective meetings.

You now understand how to monitor the energy in any meeting. You have also learned specific energy shifts to redirect meetings promptly when needed. These are core facilitation meeting skills that transform you from a rookie to a Meetings Maestro.

Practice and focus are vital to apply these skills naturally over time. Each meeting is your learning playground, whether you are a participant or a facilitator. Use them to assess the energy throughout. Observe what the facilitator does well to redirect the energy. Evaluate what does not work well. When you improve your ability to recognise the tell-tale signs of each agreement – engagement zone, you will fast-track your facilitation skills.

Make sure you practice different energy shifts. Distinguish between messy and elegant shifts and start building a repository of shifts that work well for you.

After starting and leading a meeting well, now you need to close strong too. The next chapter will teach you how to end your meeting on a high.

NOTES

1 "Steve Jobs Biography," Business News Daily, accessed on 15 June, 2021, https://www.businessnewsdaily.com/4195-business-profile-steve-jobs.html

2 Neil A. Bradbury, "Attention span during lectures: 8 seconds, 10 minutes, or more?" Chicago Medical School, accessed 17 June, 2021, https://journals.physiology.org/doi/pdf/10.1152/advan.00109.2016

3 Stephen R. Covey, The 7 Habits of Highly Effective People (Pocket Books, 2004), 235-237.

4 Brené Brown, Dare to Lead (Vermilion, 2018), 56.

7 END ON A HIGH

DEFINE CLEAR AND AGREED NEXT STEPS AND OWNERSHIP

Every two years, the Summer or Winter Olympic Games are held to celebrate the world's best athletes in a riveting competition. I love the Olympics. Sports run deeply across the DNA of my family. We would watch as much footage as possible and cheer for our favourites. The 16-day event always finishes with a majestic closing ceremony. The purpose of the closing ceremony is to acknowledge the participants as well as look ahead to the host city of the next Olympic Games that will take over the symbolic Olympic Flame.

The closing ceremony is meaningful in two important ways. First, it signals there is something else to look forward to despite the end of the event. Also, it celebrates the amazing efforts that athletes, volunteers, and organisers put into a successful event.

Equally, successful meetings can benefit from a similar ending. Imagine you are at the end of a meeting. The clock is ticking, and there are just a few minutes left in your meeting. Your participants might be tuning out already. Perhaps they are thinking about the next thing on their agenda: a well-deserved break, another meeting, or a different activity.

If you fail to close strongly, precious time is wasted, and attendees are left with a bitter aftertaste.

You need to keep control and make the most of these final minutes to end on a high. If you fail to close strongly, precious time is wasted, and attendees are left with a bitter aftertaste. Instead, ensure that the levels of agreement and engagement continue beyond your meeting and result in action and real progress.

Exceptional meetings achieve outcomes and foster improved relationships between participants to take collaboration and results to the next level. So, wrap up by conducting a mini-closing ceremony that ensures lasting meeting progress:

1. Save time by reviewing and sending out meeting minutes with your attendees.
2. Boost team spirit by appreciating specific contributions from attendees.

Leave a great aftertaste and pave the way to progress.

SAVE TIME BY REVIEWING/SENDING OUT MEETING MINUTES

"Are you kidding me, how is this possible?", I told my colleague a few years ago. I had just come back from holiday. During my leave, my team had an important meeting with a senior stakeholder. The purpose of the session was to agree on the best way forward for our project. We had formulated three alternative strategies and recommended one of them. Upon my return, my colleague told me that the stakeholder wanted us to go forward with our recommendation. Then, when I checked in later with the stakeholder, it seemed she preferred a completely different approach. I could not believe how the agreed approach was somehow lost in translation between the participants.

Failure to walk away with an agreed-upon interpretation is more than just a waste. Goodwill and connection also take a big hit.

This is the worst thing that can happen after a meeting. Disagreement between participants about next steps and ownership. Precious time and energy are invested in meetings. Failure to walk away with an agreed-upon interpretation is more than just a waste. Goodwill and connection also take a big hit.

The only solution is to invest more time to clarify the exact next steps. Doing something that was already done, but poorly captured. Meeting minutes are the solution. Quality meeting minutes capture and socialise clear action items with the right audience. But what makes for great meeting minutes?

Consideration #1: What makes great meeting minutes

In my consulting days, I worked with organisations that captured every single word that was said in meeting minutes. There are a few problems with this approach. One person is just writing things down for the whole meeting, and not everything that is said is relevant to be captured. Also, more review is required to ensure key people are comfortable with the final notes. The length of these minutes delays the review process.

At worst, meeting minutes are not captured and shared at all. Individual participants make notes, but there is no consolidation process to ensure people are aligned. Here, the problem is that people interpret notes differently, especially over time. A different interpretation results in disagreement on actual next steps.

Purposeful meeting minutes are an invaluable summary of agreed decisions and action items. This summary ensures everyone is on the same page. Also, it simplifies the process of tracking the status of the agreed actions. Meeting minutes are complete when both context and agreements are summarised.

Context includes the why, what, who, and when. Agreements include key decisions and agreed-upon tasks and ownership of those tasks.

There are ground rules to define agreed actions and allocate task ownership in the best possible way. These rules improve understanding of what was agreed to specifically and maximise the chance that tasks are completed in the shortest possible time.

Ground Rules for Great Action Items

- Each action item is owned by a single person.
- The owner of each action was present at the meeting.
- Each action item has a clear and specific target completion date.
- Each action item has a target completion date within the next month.
- Define action items with specific language to avoid confusion.

Each action is owned by a single person.

Make it clear who is responsible for completing each action item.

The owner of each action was present at the meeting.

It is possible that you need help from someone outside the attendees. For example, a senior stakeholder needs to escalate a particular issue. If that person was not present, allocate someone who was present with the task to raise this issue with the relevant stakeholder.

Track key decisions under the key decisions section in your meeting minutes and track them in relevant project management tools used by your team / organisation.

Each action item has a clear and specific target completion date.

Clarity is key to ensure a sense of urgency and priority for action owners. Dates need to be clear. Avoid things like 'by May 2021', 'next week'. Instead, dictate specific date like '15 May 2021', 'by 5 p.m. on Friday 12 November', and so forth.

Each action item has a target completion date within the next month.

For action items to be effective, they need a sense of urgency. Set them for completion within the month ahead. If the completion date is further into the future, decide whether the task should be broken down into a single or multiple tasks that can be completed in the next few weeks to ensure progress sooner rather than later.

Track bigger milestones as part of your key decisions and in relevant project management tools used by your team / organisation.

Define action items with specific language to avoid confusion.

Specific language is key to ensure people are on the same page. For example, if the action is to prepare a strategy document, ensure that people know what template to use to avoid disappointment and unnecessary re-work later on.

Simple words that define a clear 'see, hear, feel'-experience are best, rather than ambiguous words that mean different things to people. For example, 'email John Smith from the Finance Team to obtain written confirmation of the budget for project X' is clearer than 'obtain budget confirmation for our project'.

Use these ground rules to capture the best possible minutes in your future meetings. You can also use my meeting minute template to simplify this process without reinventing the wheel:

CONTEXT	
WHY (Specific Purpose)	*to inform / improve / decide / persuade*
WHAT (Objectives)	*1)*
	2)
	3)
WHO (Attendees)	*Names and roles*
WHEN	

MEETING MINUTES	
KEY DECISIONS	
AGREED TASKS & OWNERSHIP	***Person ABCD** will do **ABCD by Date ABDCD***

Ensure that this template is finalised and agreed upon prior to the end of the meeting with all participants

To make this process easy, follow the approach I learned from my former colleague Kwabena Bediako. At the end of a meeting, Kwabena would simply hit 'reply all' on the original calendar invite and add in the key decisions, agreed tasks, and ownership. When your meeting invite is properly set up with the context, this approach keeps all information linked and in one place for your audience. If needed, you can add your decisions and activities to project management tools used by your organisation to ensure they still are front of mind.

Consideration #2: When to agree and share meeting minutes

Meeting minutes are not rocket science. There is no need to polish them over a prolonged period. Attendees benefit from minutes that are released as soon as possible. Then, actions can be completed at once. Decisions and agreed actions are fresh in mind during the meeting. Afterward, our memory fades as other events take place. Even the interpretation of our notes can change over time.

Benefit by having a designated person capture minutes on the fly during the meeting and agree to them before leaving the meeting. Use the final moments to review a summary of action items and decisions and ensure that everyone is on the same page. With the increase of online meetings, a useful practice is to share the minutes on the screen. Each person can read the minutes and propose changes if needed. Once everyone is on board, simply send out the minutes directly by emailing all participants or capturing them in your favourite project management tool.

The process of reviewing and agreeing to meeting minutes as a collective helps you build agreement across your audience.

This process prevents 'subjective minutes' based on one person's interpretation of their notes. Instead, each attendee is responsible for making sure minutes are captured well.

Core Facilitation Skill #5: Building Agreement

The process of reviewing and agreeing to meeting minutes as a collective helps you build agreement across your audience. Make sure you prepare accordingly to reserve time upfront for this process. Ideally, capture this in your flow. In her book, *Dare to Lead*[1], American research professor Dr. Brené Brown, shares a particular practice embedded in her team meetings: a bell will sound 10 minutes prior to the end of the meeting to signal that it is time to wrap up the discussion and review the next steps. You can apply a similar practice, either by setting an alarm or having a designated timekeeper to keep you on track. It can be tempting to finish one more discussion item before time runs out. However, this is not worth it if the result is that minutes are not agreed with your participants. Buy-in of next steps is crucial and fosters strong accountability across your team. Instead, capture an action item for unresolved topics to obtain the relevant insights at a later stage, either through a meeting or via reply email if appropriate.

By applying this process, you save time, capture a clear track record of next steps, and ensure all participant are on the same page.

Action Items

Save time by reviewing/sending out meeting minutes

Avoid misinterpretation of next steps and wasted time.

Practice Core Facilitation Skill #5: Building Agreement:

Reserve time at the end of your meeting to ensure all participants are on the same page.

During the meeting:

- *Use the meeting minutes template to summarise the meeting context and agreements.*
- *Use the ground rules to define specific action items with clear ownership and a target completion date.*
- *Reserve time at the end of your meeting to share the minutes and refine them based on feedback, ensuring that all participants are on board.*

Meetings are a waste of time unless clear actions are agreed to by all participants to make progress.

BOOST TEAM SPIRIT BY APPRECIATING SPECIFIC CONTRIBUTIONS FROM ATTENDEES

In 1993, Israeli psychologist and economist Daniel Kahneman and his research partners conducted an interesting experiment.

They investigated how people compared two different negative experiences. In the first experience, participants submerged one hand for 60 seconds in chilly water with a temperature of 14 degrees Celsius. In the second experience, participants submerged the other hand in cold water for 90 seconds. In the first minute, the water temperature was 14 degrees Celsius, but in the remaining 30 seconds the temperature was gradually increased to 15 degrees Celsius. Participants then were asked which of the two experiences they preferred[2].

Along with first impressions and strong negative or positive peaks throughout a particular event, last impressions matter.

The majority preferred the second experience, being exposed to cold water over a longer period. The temperature increase was considered a more favourable end compared to the first experiment. Kahneman summarised his findings in the appropriately titled essay 'When more pain is preferred than less: adding a better end'. The phenomenon was called the 'peak-end rule'.

Along with first impressions and strong negative or positive peaks throughout a particular event, last impressions matter. They impact how people remember that experience over time. In other words, last impressions live on in our memory. The peak-end experience plays a significant role in shaping our memory and examples can be found for either positive or negative endings.

For example, imagine your favourite team losing a game in the final minutes. Despite a great performance throughout, you will have a bitter aftertaste of disappointment. On the other hand, imagine attending a music concert with a mediocre performance. However, if the artist finishes by playing some of your all-time favourite songs, you will walk away with a more positive experience of the event.

End on a high with your own peak-end experience

The peak-end experience is a powerful tool. So, put it to practice in meetings and end on a high.

A poor meeting end is when you are stuck in a heated discussion in the final minutes. This is a challenging moment. Many facilitators are unsure how to continue. Should you jump in and stop the discussion to wrap on time? Or should you let it go just a bit longer in the hope that it magically finished on time? By allowing discussions to continue, the meeting will go over time. Or worse, participants may suddenly leave due to other commitments. In either scenario, there is no time to agree next steps and end on a high.

Manage time as best as possible to be respectful and wrap up on time. Of course, it is possible that certain agenda items will take more time than expected. If that is the case and there are only five minutes left, decide to pause the discussion and shift gears. Use the remaining time to agree on next steps with all participants present. If needed, capture any unresolved items in the next steps or set up more time for discussion at a later stage.

To end on a high, schedule time before the end of the meeting to review and agree on meeting minutes with your attendees. This process boosts the level of agreement between the attendees about what is next.

However, there is more you can do. The primary objective of meetings is to agree on next steps that pave the way to progress and exceptional team performance. A secondary objective is to strengthen team spirit wherever possible. Use the final minutes to create your own meeting peak-end experience and end on a high through appreciation:

Core Facilitation Skill #6 – Appreciating Attendees

Each person on this planet wants to feel appreciated, be listened to, and receive recognition for their contributions. Whether you contributed a little or a lot, hearing genuine and specific appreciation is always a wonderful experience. Apply this to your meetings and appreciate your attendees. The best time is at the end of the meeting after you have agreed to the minutes.

Share what specific contributions from others you genuinely appreciated during the meeting:

What you can appreciate in others	Explanation and examples
TIME INVESTED	At a minimum, your attendees invested time to attend the meeting. Perhaps they also spent time on travel and preparation for a productive session. • *Thank you for joining us today.*
MEETING ROLES	Each role played by participants should be acknowledged. Timekeeper, facilitator, presenter, and so forth. • *Thank you [name] for keeping us on time today.* • *Thank you [name] for presenting the findings.* • *And so forth.*
SPECIFIC CONTRIBUTIONS	During the discussion, attendees shared specific ideas and questions to bring the meeting to life and achieve the objectives. • *Thank you [name] for asking critical questions around the viability of this project.* • *Thank you [name] for your enthusiasm in sharing many great ideas today.* • *And so forth.*

Opportunities for appreciation are abundant. But not all types of appreciation are effective. There is a clear line between genuine contribution and trying to tick a box with a generic compliment. People can feel the difference. To boost team spirit, be specific and genuine when you appreciate each person individually. Frequent, heartfelt appreciation and positive reinforcement strengthens individual and team relationships. Ultimately, better relationships create better outcomes.

In larger meetings, appreciating each person may not be possible. In that case, it is acceptable to acknowledge a group of people in one go. But if you can, share appreciation with each attendee to benefit from the peak end experience as much as possible.

Inspiration for creating your own peak-end experience

Some organisations take this practice to the next level. For example, The Elevation Company has a special practice in which team meetings finish with each participant sharing a quick acknowledgement. A great practice to get everyone involved and boost team spirit.

I always wrap up my workshops with a special activity called 'pegs of acknowledgement', which I learned from my former colleague Heather Yelland, director of The Elevation Company. To introduce the activity, I share the importance of saying thanks and appreciating others. This simple yet powerful practice is often neglected by organisations and people in general. The best appreciation is done in a memorable way. So, I tell my audience about the pegs of acknowledgement or, as I like to call them, 'Medals of acknowledgement and appreciation'.

> *Be creative and end on a high with a crescendo. Your attendees will love it!*

I hand out laundry pegs to all participants and ask them to think of someone who impressed them in some way, either during the workshop or in general in their team. Then, I ask participants to write the words that best describe the attitude, energy, or behaviours of that person on the laundry peg. Once done, it is time to put appreciation to practice. Participants walk up to the person they wrote about, and then clip on their 'medal'. I ask participants to look the other person in the eye and clearly tell them what they appreciate and value. To set the scene, I play 'Celebration' by Kool and the Gang in the background, which contributes to a fun and festive atmosphere. I love the pegs of acknowledgement exercise: it is so much fun! You can feel how team spirit grows because of these celebratory interactions. Once done, participants often come up to me and ask for more pegs. They enjoyed the process so much and want to repeat it with as many people in their team as possible.

You can feel how team spirit grows because of these celebratory interactions.

Be creative and end on a high with a crescendo. Your attendees will love it!

Action Items

Boost team spirit by appreciating specific contributions from attendees

Be respectful, finish meetings on time and end on a high!

Whilst the primary purpose of meetings is to achieve your objectives, the secondary purpose is to strengthen the connection with your attendees.

Practice Core Facilitation Skill #6: Appreciating Attendees:

Tell your attendees what you value in them.

After you have agreed the meeting minutes:

Thank your participants for their time, specific roles played, and contributions shared.

Name participants individually.

Be genuine and specific.

End meetings on a high.

Reflect:

- *How did you feel after appreciating your attendees?*
- *What will you do less / differently / more of in future meetings?*
- *What else did you learn from this practice?*

IN A NUTSHELL

Even if your meeting has been productive until the final minutes, you cannot take the end of a meeting for granted. Instead, be respectful, finish on time, and end on a high. A Meetings Maestro is in control from start to finish.

Reserve time to review and agree on key decisions, next steps, and ownership with your attendees. This simple practice avoids misinterpretation of what to do next. Instead, everyone is on the same page. From here, there is a clear action plan to progress.

Meetings should be about more than just agreeing to actions. By investing the final minutes to appreciate your participants, you benefit from the 'peak-end rule' and boost team spirit. Last impressions count. You need to feel valued and appreciated like all humans. Use public, genuine, and specific appreciation for each attendee and feel the positive shift in team energy.

By applying these steps, you deliver meetings that achieve outcomes and end on a high.

In the next and last section, learn how to make your learnings stick and create a plan for continuous improvement. The pathway to progress is a process of continuous learning. By putting this process into practice, you reap the benefits of growth and leadership opportunities.

NOTES

1 Brené Brown, Dare to Lead (Vermilion, 2018), 54-55.

2 Daniel Kahneman, Barbara L. Fredrickson, Charles A. Schreiber, Donald A. Redelmeier, "When More Pain Is Preferred to Less: Adding a Better End," accessed on 4 June, 2021, https://journals.sagepub.com/doi/10.1111/j.1467-9280.1993.tb00589.x

PART 2 – DELIVER

PART 3 – DEVELOP

BECOME A MEETINGS MAESTRO FASTER

8 PRACTICE INTENTIONALLY

THE THREE-STEP PROCESS TO BECOME BETTER, FASTER

Mathematics was a major subject throughout my life in school. I learned the first basics in primary school. In high school, things got trickier with basic geometry and algebra. When I enrolled for a degree of Industrial Engineering & Management, I started to learn advanced calculus. What a tough nut to crack! Overall, I spent perhaps hundreds of hours over 20 years learning different elements of mathematics. You would think that after such an extended study period, I should still be a mathematical wizard. Far from it. I doubt that I would pass any of the exams I nailed 15 years ago.

If you don't use it, you lose it.

In contrast, consider driving a car. I was a slow learner, and I failed my driving test twice. I finally obtained my Dutch driver's license when I was 22 years old. Learning how to drive can be daunting. There is the preparation before driving: adjusting the steering wheel, mirrors, and seat if needed. Then, driving itself requires constant focus and use of different tools in parallel. Experienced drivers use the steering wheel, gas and brake pedals, and gearbox naturally. Inexperienced drivers need time and focus. Driving can be overwhelming at first. But with frequent practice, it becomes easier and more natural.

It is up to you how fast you will become a Meetings Maestro who delivers 'on the money'-meetings consistently and helps colleagues uplift their meeting game too.

If you do use it, you keep it!

So far, you have learned a success recipe for how to schedule meetings smarter, and you have learned the core facilitation skills required to lead meetings that achieve outcomes. Now, it is up to you how fast you will become a Meetings Maestro who delivers 'on the money'-meetings consistently and helps colleagues uplift their meeting game too.

This chapter will help you create a tangible action plan so that you can progress faster. There are three key steps to accelerate your growth:

1. **Reflect** – Identify what you can do differently to facilitate better meetings.
2. **Realign** – Prioritise specific areas of improvement to make the biggest impact.

3. **Realise** – Reap the benefits from putting your learnings quickly into practice.

If you use this process, you are in control of your growth. Instead of missing out, you accelerate your journey on the rookie-to-maestro spectrum. Then, you reap the real benefits of saving time and delivering better outcomes.

REFLECT – IDENTIFY WHAT YOU CAN DO DIFFERENTLY TO FACILITATE BETTER MEETINGS

After heavy World War II losses, Japan needed to rebuild its country and economy. Several foreign experts provided support in the effort. One of them was American statistician and professor Dr. W. Edward Deming. Deming helped with statistical control to improve the quality of manufacturing facilities. Over time, the 'Kaizen' philosophy was born. Kaizen means 'change is good' and indicates that there is always room for improvement. American life and business strategist Anthony Robbins uses a similar philosophy in his seminars under a different term: 'CANI', short for 'Constant and Never-ending Improvement'.

When you have completed your meeting, it can be tempting to complete other actions. This is not bad. However, it is a missed opportunity.

When you have completed your meeting, it can be tempting to complete other actions. This is not bad. However, it is a missed CANI opportunity. It is not talent that separates 'the best' from 'the average', regardless of the field. 'The best' review what went well and what could have gone better. Then, they define and apply an action plan for continuous improvement.

Make sure you do not get stuck on a hamster wheel of doing the same things repeatedly. Things will not improve. Now that you have learned the Design and Deliver methods, you need to do two things:

1. Put your learnings to practice as soon as possible.
2. Reflect on what you can do differently to facilitate even better meetings.

When it comes to reflection, there are three critical sources of insights.

Source 1: Self-Assessment

Self-awareness is an important skill and the starting point for your reflection. Consider your end-to-end meeting, from preparation to delivery, and evaluate what worked well and what could have gone better. Use the Design principles and Core Facilitation Skills as a guide. Some people focus on what went well, others on what could have gone better. However, a self-assessment needs to be balanced. So, acknowledge strengths and areas for improvement. Write down your observations to get the best results. This creates a track record of your progress over time.

> *Self-awareness is an important skill and the starting point for your reflection.*

Source 2: Feedback from attendees

Your attendees have experienced the end-to-end meeting process first-hand. They have received your invite and participated in the session. Ask for feedback to obtain invaluable insights that you might have missed in your self-assessment.

If you want, you can ask every attendee for feedback. However, feel free to ask one or two people you trust most. Tell them you are working on your skills and that you would like to receive their thoughts to identify growth areas. Like with your self-assessment, obtain a balanced view of what you did well and what you could do better.

Source 3: Mentor

Mentors are a great resource for insights too. Ideal mentors are people who have already developed the skills you seek to develop, so they can guide you well. Also, a great mentor is someone who genuinely cares about your success with whom you easily connect.

Ideal mentors are people who have already developed the skills you seek to develop.

Mentors can make an enormous difference. They provide positive guidance and a gentle nudge for accountability so that you can progress faster. So, consider who might be a great person to help you out.

To make the most of your mentor arrangement, schedule regular catch-ups and help your mentor understand your struggles and give examples of how you approached certain situations and ask for feedback and guidance.

Insights from all three sources provide you with a wide range of feedback to identify what you can do differently to facilitate better meetings. Next, it is time to prioritise specific focus areas to work on.

ACTION ITEMS

Reflect – Identify what you can do differently to facilitate better meetings.

Each meeting is a learning opportunity. Apply CANI: Continuous and Never-ending Improvement!

Invest time to reflect and identify strengths and areas for improvement.

Obtain insights from:

1. *Self-assessment*
2. *Feedback from others*
3. *Mentor*

See the 'Become a Meetings Maestro today' section at the end of this book with instructions on how to access a free reflection worksheet.

REALIGN – PRIORITISE SPECIFIC AREAS OF IMPROVEMENT THAT WILL MAKE THE BIGGEST DIFFERENCE

Earlier in this book, I shared how I did a trial class in Wing Chun Kungfu late 2018. I quickly fell in love with the martial art. Over the last few years, I ramped up my training to progress through the first grades. Then, I had the opportunity to sign up for the academy's instructor's course. I loved the idea of being able to fast-track my skills and teach beginners basic moves. Just prior to Christmas 2020, I completed the course and achieved the rank of trainee instructor. Since then, I teach one class each week to our Grade 1 students.

Feedback plays a significant role in teaching. The challenge is how much feedback to give. I was tempted to give a lot of feedback to my students to help them improve quicker. However, a high volume of feedback is overwhelming. Instead, one or two areas for improvement are digestible for students.

The same holds true for improving your design and delivery of meetings. You may be looking at a laundry list of items from your reflection exercise. Instead of focusing on everything, it is time to prioritise specific areas of improvement that will make the biggest difference.

Romanian American engineer Joseph Juran was a pioneer in quality-control management. In the early 1950s, Juran discovered the Pareto principle, also known as '80/20'. In the context of quality control, he discovered that 80% of issues was caused by only 20% of the issues[1]. By resolving these causes, Juran helped organisations like General Motors fast-track their quality and organisational performance.

To become a better facilitator faster, you need to adopt a mindset of continuous improvement and apply your realisations quickly.

Similarly, apply the Pareto principle when it comes to improving your meeting skills.

Review your list of improvements. Assess which ones will have the biggest impact on your ability to deliver exceptional meetings and re-order your list accordingly. Once done, you can highlight the top-20% of areas for improvement at the top and prioritise those for improvement.

In 2013, American authors and entrepreneurs Gary Keller and Jay Papasan publish their book, The ONE Thing: The Surprisingly Simple Truth Behind Extraordinary Results[2]. The book teaches how an elaborate 'to do'-list is both overwhelming and unproductive. Instead, the authors challenge readers to adopt a different approach when it comes to getting things done smarter. To help, they suggest the 'Focusing Question':

"What's the ONE Thing I can do such that by doing it everything else will be easier or unnecessary?"

Benefit from the one thing approach. Now that you have prioritised specific areas for improvement, ask yourself:

'What is the one thing I can do differently either in the lead up to my meeting or at the start of my meeting that by doing so, will make my next meeting much more effective and powerful?'

To become a better facilitator faster, you need to adopt a mindset of continuous improvement and apply your realisations quickly. If you make each meeting just 1% better than the previous one, over the course of a year you will be twice as good at running meetings as before. Keep in mind that the 'Pareto Principle' and 'Focusing Question' practice can help you become a lot better and faster than that.

Action Items

Realign - Prioritise specific areas of improvement that will make the biggest difference

Adopt the 'Pareto Principle' and 'Focusing Question' to identify the biggest impact areas for improvement.

For each meeting use your findings from your reflection and:

- *Assess which ones will have the biggest impact on your ability to deliver exceptional meetings and re-order your list accordingly.*
- *Ask: What is the one thing you can do that will have the biggest impact of addressing the biggest area of improvement?*

Next, it is time to apply your realisations quickly.

REALISE – REAP THE BENEFITS BY IMPLEMENTING LEARNINGS QUICKLY

Have you ever had a great idea but never acted on it? It happens to all of us. Life can get in the way and distract us with urgent matters or disruptions.

Progress only happens at the intersection of inspiration and implementation.

Inspiration comes from many places. Conversations with others, watching a TED talk, reading a book, or even a random thought could bring about a great idea. However, without implementation, inspiration is just a dream. Implementation is where the rubber hits the road. It is about action. But, just doing things for the sake of being busy does not lead to progress. That is like being stuck on a hamster wheel without pursuing novel ideas.

Progress is about bringing together both inspiration and implementation.

This book is full of ideas that can help you design and deliver exceptional meetings that deliver results and bring people closer together. Equally, your identified list of improvements for your next meeting is inspiration.

Now, it is time to put them to practice. Nothing changes if nothing changes. So, apply your realisations from reflect and realign so that you can realise growth and better results.

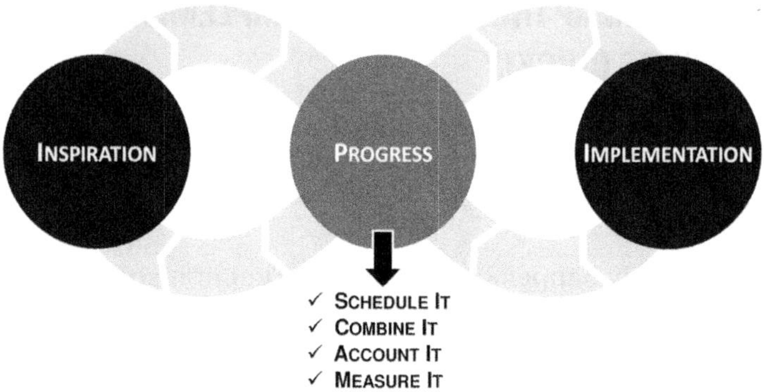

American author James Clear published his excellent book *Atomic Habits: Tiny Changes, Remarkable Results in 2018.*[3] Based on this work, there are some things you can do to make this new practice a habit:

Consideration #1: Schedule it – what gets scheduled, gets done!

'Time-blocking' is a popular time management tool to prioritise important tasks. By scheduling in time to review your meetings, you make progress inevitable rather than leaving it to chance.

Consideration #2: Combine it – batch logical tasks together for win-wins!

Rather than scheduling new time in the calendar, you can save time by batching new ideas together with existing practices that naturally fit. For example, my friend Jonathan conducts a weekly planning session on Sunday evenings to prepare for the week ahead. If you have a similar practice, you can add the reflect-re-align-realise process as a fitting add-on.

Consideration #3: Account it – have someone keep you on the hook!

Appoint someone to act as your accountability partner. When others are checking in on progress, people are more likely to follow through on goals and intentions. Similarly, buddy up with a colleague and keep each other accountable for greater team growth and performance. This is also a great method to bounce off ideas and grow faster together, so that everyone benefits.

Consideration #4: Measure it – make progress visible!

Without keeping a record, it is difficult to know how much you have grown over time. By writing down strengths and areas for improvement along with keeping a repository of audience feedback, you create evidence of your growth journey. You will notice how areas of improvement become strengths and new growth areas appear. This record also helps you to prioritise recurring areas for development if needed.

The extent to which you become a better facilitator faster is up to you. Practice combined with the reflect-realign-realise process make perfect. Progress will not occur unless you implement your learnings.

Action Items

Realise - Reap the benefits by implementing learnings quickly

Apply your learnings to become a better facilitator faster.
Progress occurs at the intersection of inspiration and implementation.

Use the progress considerations to make the reflect-realign-realise process a habit and reap the benefits:

- *Schedule it – what gets scheduled, gets done!*
- *Combine it – batch logical tasks together for win-wins!*
- *Account it – have someone keep you on the hook!*
- *Measure it – make progress visible!*

Do the following:

1. *Schedule a time in your calendar to review your progress at least weekly for 15 minutes or combine this review with other reflection time you already have as a habit.*
2. *Reach out to someone to keep you on the hook and accountable.*
3. *Give yourself a score (1 = poor, 5 = expert) against the meeting design principles and core facilitation skills to measure where you are today and make your progress visible over time.*
4. *Make an action plan to keep on reviewing the core elements of this book as you progress your learnings*

IN A NUTSHELL

Rome was not built in one day. Practice makes perfect. In this last chapter, you have learned the fundamental steps required to practice intentionally, so that you can become a better facilitator faster.

Progress is about finding inspiration in things you can do differently to create better results. But without putting this inspiration to practice, you will be stuck on a hamster wheel: doing the same things over and over again.

Remember, it is insanity to expect different results without changing your approach.

To develop an exceptional meetings culture where 'on the money'-meetings become the norm, you need to use the process outlined in this chapter with your team to foster a mindset of continuous development.

This is the process that will enable you to progress faster from rookie to Meetings Maestro and help you to be able to consistently deliver 'on the money' meetings in the shortest possible time and help those around you uplift their meeting game too.

Without reflection, you risk sliding backwards on the spectrum. At best, 'hit n miss' meetings are the norm, and at worst, you get 'in the dark' meetings that waste time, resources, and energy.

So, commit to becoming a Meetings Maestro and doing your best to learn the Design-Deliver-Develop system and reap the benefits: stop wasting time by fixing your meetings and fixing your productivity!

NOTES

1 Joseph M. Juran and Joseph A. De Feo, Juran's Quality Handbook: The Complete Guide to Performance Excellence (The McGraw-Hill Companies, Inc., 2010), 147-150.

2 Gary Keller and Jay Papasan, The One Thing: The Surprisingly Simple Truth Behind Extraordinary Results (Bard Press, 2014), 106-108.

3 James Clear, Atomic Habits: Tiny Habits, Remarkable Results (Random House Business Books, 2018), 50-55.

PART 3 – DEVELOP

BECOME A MEETINGS MAESTRO FASTER

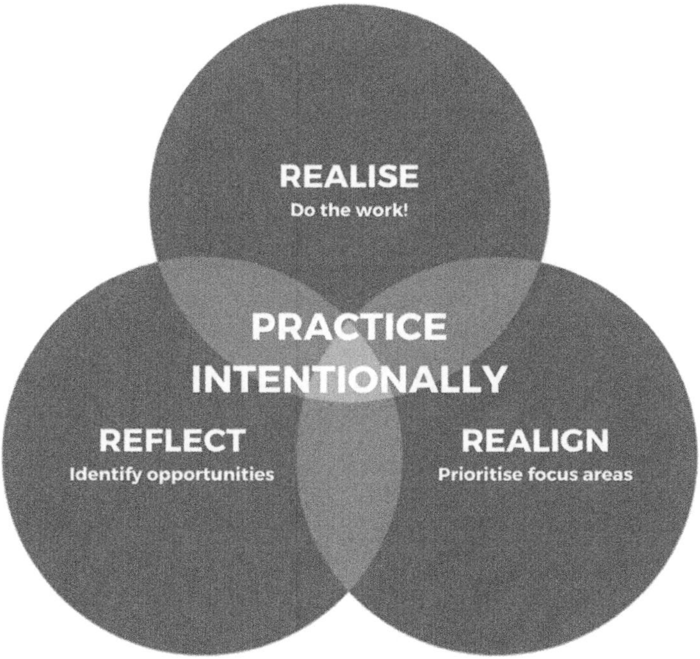

© ST Hoogwout 2020

FINAL WORDS

PUTTING MEETINGS MAESTRO TO PRACTICE

So now what? You have finished this book. You get it. You are ready to conduct engaging, purposeful, and effective meetings. Where do you start?

FOR INDIVIDUALS

The easiest way to approach meetings is in three steps: before, during, and after.

1. **Before**: Think through each of the 9 design elements before you schedule a meeting.
2. **During**: Keep things easy by focusing on improving one of the core facilitation skills.
3. **After**: Reflect what went well and what could have gone better in your meeting.

Remember, practice makes perfect.

FOR TEAMS

Make progress by sharing the Design-Deliver-Develop system with your team. Digging into Meetings Maestro together gives your team a shared language and understanding how exceptional meetings can help everyone in your organisation.

1. **Learn**: Distribute copies of this book across your team and collectively read a chapter weekly.
2. **Reflect**: Reflect on your key takeaways from each chapter.
3. **Agree**: Discuss and agree on how to put everyone's learnings into practice.

Keep in mind that it takes more than reading the book and a few discussions to make exceptional meetings the norm. Practice consistently and help others to reinforce a shared commitment to conducting engaging, purposeful, and effective meetings across your organisation.

BECOME A MEETINGS MAESTRO TODAY!

Now that you understand the theory, it is time to put Meetings Maestro into action in your life. Visit my website to continue your journey! Find up-to-date information on my seminars and coaching programs, as well as digital copies of the Meetings Maestro tools mentioned in this book:

- Self-assessment
- Meeting invite template
- Meeting flow template
- Meeting minutes template
- Soft copies of each of the diagrams in this book

Visit https://sthoogwout.com.au/meetings-maestro today!

ABOUT THE AUTHOR

Siebe-Thijs (ST) Hoogwout provides consulting and personal effectiveness training to a wide variety of clients, from private sector organisations to government agencies and non-for-profits. A large focus of his work is helping executives boost team productivity and cohesion.

His unique way of approaching team development comes from ST's diverse path as a husband, management consultant, martial arts instructor, youth camp volunteer, orchestra musician, and even DJ over the last two decades.

ST has a master's degree in Industrial Engineering and Management from Twente University in the Netherlands and a master's degree in International Business from Sydney University in Australia. He has fifteen years of management consulting experience and ten years of experience in training and development. The last five years have been devoted to designing and leading programs that enhance individual and group performance within large organisations with a focus on conversational team-building exercises that bring people closer together and help them live a fulfilled life.

In his spare time, ST loves hiking, practising Wing Chun Kung Fu, enjoying a variety of (live) music, and reading memoirs. He lives with his wife, Mariam, in Sydney, Australia.

ACKNOWLEDGEMENTS

Wow, the last 12 months have been an incredible rollercoaster full of learning experiences for me! To write a book is rewarding but incredibly challenging. This book would have remained an intangible idea if it were not for several phenomenal people.

To my wonderful wife Mariam, the love of my life. Every day together is a wonderful gift; thank you for your ongoing love and support. You have helped me so much in making this book become a beautiful reality: from teaching me Canva for design, photographing me live in action at workshops as well as countless headshots, through to incredible design advice on selecting the best artists, colour-schemes and so forth. Thank you, I love you!

To my parents, mama and papa, you have given me and my siblings so much. You have always supported me without shying away from difficult talks when needed, to make sure I would follow the best possible path in life. Thank you for your support to help me immigrate to Australia – I cannot imagine how difficult this might have been for you. I am also grateful for your suggestions over the last few months to make this book better. Thank you for your love, support, and wisdom. I love you.

To my beautiful baby daughter, I cannot wait to meet you when you come into this world in a few months. May this book be a wonderful reminder that you can achieve your dreams too, as long as you persevere and surround yourself with an amazing group of loved ones and advisors for support.

A special thanks goes to Shani Raja. Thank you for your friendship, generosity, and wisdom! It is rare to meet someone who so selflessly and genuinely offers their time to help others. I am forever grateful for our catchups that so often turned into mentoring sessions, particularly our 90-minute brainstorm session for the title of this book.

When I started to write this book, I was completely overwhelmed. I did not know where to start. Thanks to Kath Walter's structured 'Overnight Authority' writing process and guidance along the way, I was able to embark on a clear roadmap to make this book a reality. Thanks, Kath.

To Jeffery Wang, Julie Bowden, Jack de Leeuw, Sankshep Vashisht and Sue Woodall. Thank you for taking the time to read my first manuscript and offering brilliant feedback. Your kind words and continued support mean the world to me.

Over the years, I have been blessed to work with a diverse group of amazing clients, partners, and colleagues. Thank you for trusting me and my passion. You bring out the best in me and I look forward to continue to supporting you!

To my editor Douglas Williams. Thank you for your comprehensive feedback to improve and tighten the flow and structure of this book. It has been a pleasure to work with you and transform the rough manuscript into a polished end result. To Ralph Angelo Monares, for the incredible chapter illustrations, and to Ryan Urz for the slick book cover.

Over the years, I have been influenced by so many teachers and my thinking will always evolve as I learn more. To all of those who have gone before and imparted their wisdom on me, knowingly or unknowingly, thank you!

And to all my friends and family. Thank you for your support and love throughout the years. Without you, I would not be who I am today.

Onwards and upwards!

Siebe-Thijs Hoogwout